Lab Reports and Projects in
Sport and Exercise Science

PEARSON

At Pearson, we take learning personally. Our courses and resources are available as books, online and via multi-lingual packages, helping people learn whatever, wherever and however they choose.

We work with leading authors to develop the strongest learning experiences, bringing cutting-edge thinking and best learning practice to a global market. We craft our print and digital resources to do more to help learners not only understand their content, but to see it in action and apply what they learn, whether studying or at work.

Pearson is the world's leading learning company. Our portfolio includes Penguin, Dorling Kindersley, the Financial Times and our educational business, Pearson International. We are also a leading provider of electronic learning programmes and of test development, processing and scoring services to educational institutions, corporations and professional bodies around the world.

Every day our work helps learning flourish, and wherever learning flourishes, so do people.

To learn more please visit us at: www.pearson.com/uk

Lab Reports and Projects in Sport and Exercise Science

A Guide for Students

Mike Price

Harlow, England • London • New York • Boston • San Francisco • Toronto • Sydney
Auckland • Singapore • Hong Kong • Tokyo • Seoul • Taipei • New Delhi
Cape Town • São Paulo • Mexico City • Madrid • Amsterdam • Munich • Paris • Milan

Pearson Education Limited
Edinburgh Gate
Harlow CM20 2JE
United Kingdom
Tel: +44 (0)1279 623623
Web: www.pearson.com/uk

First published 2013 (print and electronic)

ISBN: 978-0-273-75840-2 (print)
        978-0-273-75844-0 (PDF)
        978-0-273-77970-4 (eText)

British Library Cataloguing-in-Publication Data
A catalogue record for the print edition is available from the British Library

Library of Congress Cataloging-in-Publication Data
Price, Mike, 1971-
    Lab reports and projects in sport and exercise science : a guide for students / Mike Price.
        p. cm.
    Includes bibliographical references and index.
    ISBN 978-0-273-75840-2
    1. Sport sciences--Study and teaching.   2. Exercise--Study and teaching.   3. Educational reports--
Study and teaching.   I. Title.
    GV558.P75 2013
    613.71--dc23

                                                                                            2012034140

10 9 8 7 6 5 4 3 2 1
16 15 14 13 12

Print edition typeset in 10/12pt Times by 35
Print edition printed and bound in Malaysia (CTP-VP)

NOTE THAT ANY PAGE CROSS REFERENCES REFER TO THE PRINT EDITION

Dedicated to my girls, Kerri and Lilly

Contents

Publisher's acknowledgements

We are grateful to the following for permission to reproduce copyright material:

Tables

Table 2.5 from How to critically appraise an article, *Nature Clinical Practice Gastroenterology and Hepatology*, 6, pp. 82–91 (Young, J.M. and Solomons, M.J. 2009), Box 1, reprinted by permission from Macmillan Publishers Ltd; Table 2.6 adapted from READER: an acronym to aid critical reading by general practitioners, *British Journal of General Practice*, 44, pp. 83–85 (MacAuley, D. 1994), Figure 1; Table 2.7 adapted from Manuscript peer review: a helpful checklist for students and novice referees, *Advances in Physiology Education*, 23(1), pp. 52–58 (Seals, D.R. and Tanaka, H. 2000); Table 3.1 from Editorial: Keep It Simple: Study Design Nomenclature in Research Article Abstracts, *Journal of Athletic Training*, 45(3), pp. 213–214 (Hertel, J. 2000).

Text

Extract on pages 26–7 from Maximal and submaximal oxygen uptakes and blood lactate levels in elite male middle- and long-distance runners, *International Journal of Sports Medicine*, 5(5), pp. 255–61 (Svedenhag, J. and Sjodin, B. 1985), Abstract, reprinted by permission; Extract on page 27 from The ultraendurance triathlete: a physiological profile, *Medicine and Science in Sports and Exercise*, 19(1), pp. 45–50 (O'Toole, M.L., Hiller, D.B., Crosby, L.O. and Douglas, P.S. 1987), Abstract; Extract on page 28 from Changes in physical fitness parameters during a competitive field hockey season, *Journal of Strength and Conditioning Research*, 18(4), pp. 850–4 (Astorino, T.A., Tam, P.A., Rietschel, J.C., Johnson, S.M. and Freedman, T.P. 2004), Abstract; Extract on pages 28–9 from Thermoregulatory responses of spinal cord injured and able-bodied athletes to prolonged upper body exercise and recovery, *Spinal Cord*, 37(11), pp. 772–9 (Price, M.J. and Campbell, I.G. 1999), Abstract, reprinted by permission from Macmillan Publishers Ltd.

In some instances we have been unable to trace the owners of copyright material, and we would appreciate any information that would enable us to do so.

Introduction

Background to this text

The idea for this text was born one academic year when I was marking a large pile of physiology lab reports. In amongst the range of marks awarded from first class down to those just warranting a pass I found myself consistently commenting upon a range of points including errors of general report formatting, presentation of data and scientific wording. In addition, some students appeared unsure of what to include in each section of the report as well as how to adequately present and explain their results. This was even true for some students tackling their final year project. Although every student had been provided with appropriate guidance as to what was required in writing up laboratory reports there was still a general underlying lack of good report-writing skills. Although writing is a skill that develops through practice and takes time to master it became clear that it would be useful to have a recommended text that related specifically to writing lab reports. This would certainly be a good idea if it could pre-empt a considerable amount of the generic comments I was writing. Consequently, as a result of developing various tutorials, practical exercises and coursework assessments to try and improve general laboratory writing skills, it seemed reasonable to try and put them all together in one volume.

Initially the idea was to focus primarily on undergraduate laboratory reports in exercise physiology. However, it was logical to extend this concept to cover sport and exercise science more widely and also to look at writing undergraduate project dissertations. Postgraduate students embarking upon their research journeys in the form of MSc and PhD degrees may also find it useful. All of the expected outputs from such endeavours have similar underlying research processes requiring the clear reporting and explanation of the data collected. This text is certainly not intended to be a replacement for any of the excellent statistics or research design textbooks currently used alongside undergraduate curricula but should simply be used to provide guidance towards writing up scientific findings.

Throughout this text it is also not the author's intention to state what is right or wrong but to give guidance to the reader in developing their own writing style. It is also hoped that anyone using this text will gain an awareness of a range of aspects which may contribute to successful research and writing. Furthermore, it is noted regularly throughout the text that students should always seek the advice of their tutors for specific requirements with respect to their assignments. Similarly, postgraduate students should seek the advice of their research supervisors and research teams. Although postgraduate students often follow the writing style of their supervisors, due to the nature of their research relationship and the feedback provided, they also should try to develop their own personal style and approach to writing.

The structure of this text

The structure is designed to follow the sections of a typical laboratory report or dissertation; in other words: abstract, introduction/literature review, methods, results discussion and references. As such students can dip in and out of the different sections as required. Furthermore, the requirements of each report are likely to differ with the level of study and the particular assessment. Both factors need to be considered by the user. For example, first-year undergraduate students may be required to simply describe a method used and compare their data to expected responses to demonstrate an understanding of the techniques used or key underlying principles. Final-year students will have more in-depth requirements relating to generating novel research questions and hypotheses, clear research design, undertaking of appropriate statistical tests and discussion of their results in relation to previous research studies. For postgraduate students the emphasis will be on the development of and carrying out a novel research question. To this end each chapter is designed to be used independently following the needs of the student. Chapters are also organised and numbered as they would be in a conventional report.

Each chapter of the text will also try to provide an awareness of certain concepts and procedures, some of which may not be the main concern of first- or second-year students, such as ethics applications and risk assessments. Each academic establishment will have their own specific guidelines and procedures for these. Other aspects such as more advanced statistical concepts, e.g. effects size and statistical power, will be introduced. Each section will contain exercises so that students can practice various aspects of report writing. Examples will be given from key areas of sport and exercise science, such as exercise physiology, psychology and biomechanics, to illustrate various concepts. Where appropriate, each chapter will refer to three key examples of laboratory reports most students will either undertake during their studies or should at least be able to relate to, namely:

1. Measurement of maximal oxygen uptake;
2. Ground reaction forces during walking and running; and
3. The effect of arousal on performance.

Although these are not all-encompassing they do represent traditional laboratory classes undertaken by most sport and exercise scientists and may help to put each report aspect into context.

Undergraduate students

As alluded to above, the classic 'lab report' is used by many academic institutions to varying degrees and forms a significant component of your scientific training. As noted earlier, most lab reports are designed to assess the understanding and application of specific aspects of sport and exercise science and will differ depending on what the tutor is assessing. Some tutors may provide data for statistical analysis to be undertaken whereas others may use the data collected in a specific class. Your lab reports will therefore be specific to the module or unit taught and the stage you are at within your degree. Although most lab reports have the same component sections there is no substitute for following the advice and guidelines provided by your tutors as to what is required. You would be surprised at the number of times the answers to many questions are provided in the information given out by tutors early on in the academic calendar and in good time for the report to be submitted!

Postgraduate students

The final report for your postgraduate degree is generally your thesis. For masters degrees the dissertation will reflect the nature of your studies. For example, some masters degrees will have an initial taught component in the first half of the course followed by a research study in the second half of the degree (i.e. a 'Taught MSc'). Others will be predominantly research based with significantly less time spent on taught units and the main emphasis will be on the research study undertaken (i.e. a 'Masters by Research'). For PhD studies, the format of the thesis will differ depending on both the nature and area of your study. Generally the PhD thesis presents a series of studies examining key components of a larger research question. Although the end result of a PhD is to further knowledge in the research area in some way, it is more than just a thesis. A PhD is a research training, the thesis being just one – albeit large – component. Within postgraduate studies there is also a greater emphasis on publishing the results of each study as journal articles. Postgraduate students may therefore find this text useful for a number of endeavours.

However you use this text I hope that you find it useful and wish you well in your writing and studies.

Dr Mike Price

Chapter 1

Abstracts

In this chapter you will:

1.1 What is an abstract?

When you are first asked to search for or write an abstract as an undergraduate student you may well not know what your tutor is asking for. Within the context of writing, the word 'Abstract' means 'a summary' or 'an abridgement' (*Oxford English Dictionary*, 2000). Therefore, an abstract is a short summary of your work. In the context of a journal article an abstract is the first section of an article that you will see. With this in mind an abstract should provide the reader with a good idea of the key aims, general methods undertaken, the key findings and the most important take-home message. Abstracts are therefore a powerful tool in informing readers about the work that has been undertaken.

As well as abstracts being the first section of any journal article you may read they are also most likely to be the first part of a journal article that you come into contact with when undertaking a literature search. This is especially true as a result of the range of internet-based search engines with links to electronic journals that are available to today's students. When *reading* an abstract you should be able to obtain enough information to determine whether the study is related to your own research area and if it is of use to you. Alternatively, the abstract may provide you with enough information to decide that the study is not appropriate for your needs or that it is not what you thought it would be about from the title. Conversely, when *writing* an abstract it is essential to be able to clearly communicate the key points of the study to the reader.

Following the abstract there will usually be between three to ten keywords (Peh and Ng, 2008), which are used to aid search engines in their searching patterns and are usually not contained within the title. Ideally these terms should be standard terms contained within *Index Medicus* (ICMJE, 1997), which is a comprehensive index of journal titles and conventional or accepted search terms for accessing information.

1.2 Different types of abstract

When reading the literature during your studies you will come across a range of abstract types. The format of each type will depend upon whether you are writing a dissertation, a journal article or submitting your work for a conference. For undergraduate laboratory reports an abstract is not usually required, whereas for final-year projects this is an important component of the dissertation. The following sections provide an overview of the types of abstracts you are most likely to read or be asked to write.

1.2.1 Abstracts in journal articles

Within the journals you are most likely to consult there are a range of abstract formats, which differ depending on the journal's specific requirements. Some journals require a brief abstract of 100–150 words (e.g. *Journal of Sport and Exercise Psychology*) or up to 200 words (e.g. *Journal of Sports Sciences*), whereas others allow slightly longer abstracts of up to 250 (e.g. *Journal of Biomechanics*) or 275 words (e.g. *Journal of Strength and Conditioning Research*). Other journals require what is termed a 'structured abstract' with specific headings within them relating to the 'Introduction', 'Methods', 'Results' and 'Conclusions' sections of a study (e.g. *Medicine and Science in Sports and Exercise*). There may also be more specific aspects that are required such as 'Purpose', 'Study Design' (e.g. *British Journal of Sports Medicine*) or 'Outcome Measures'. Theoretically the structured abstract approach ensures certain aspects of the study design and main outcomes are clearly and consistently reported, thus aiding literature reviews and extraction of information (Squires, 1990).

The type of abstract required usually depends upon the journal you plan to submit your work to or any specific guidelines provided for your project. Either way a well-written abstract should provide all the information you need to appreciate what was done and the key findings as well as to determine whether you should read the rest of the article. Both structured and non-structured abstracts should therefore contain similar types of information. As noted earlier they usually follow the general structure of a scientific report itself, i.e. Introduction, Method, Results and Discussion, often termed the 'IMRAD' principle (Alexandrov and Hennerici, 2007; Hartley, 2000; Pamir, 2002). However, no one type of abstract is better than another as long as the key points of the work done is provided. Structured abstracts simply provide more specific prompts for content and, when reading them, they may be easier to glean key information from.

1.2.2 Abstracts in dissertations

Abstracts for dissertations are essentially the same as those for journal articles in that they inform the reader of what was done and the key findings. Abstracts are not usually presented within laboratory reports, however, so you should consult your coursework guidelines as to what your tutor expects. Just as abstracts will differ between journals the requirements of universities and colleges for dissertation abstracts also differ. In general, abstracts for dissertations will have either a specific word length (e.g. 500 words) or should fit comfortably onto one page (approximately 300 words for Times Roman, font size 12 and double-spaced text).

1.2.3 Abstracts for conferences

A further form of abstract is that of abstracts submitted to conferences. The majority of researchers will endeavour to present their research findings at a conference or other scientific meeting in order to disseminate their work. This provides a range of networking and feedback opportunities and is often one of the initial goals for post-graduate students prior to submitting their work as a journal article for publication. For a researcher's work to be accepted for presentation at a conference, whether as an oral presentation or as a scientific poster, authors will have to submit an abstract. As for journal articles the submitted abstract will undergo a peer-review process. Peer review involves a number of reviewers assessing the content of the abstract. If it is of the desired standard and relevant to the theme of the conference, then it may be accepted for presentation.

As with journal articles there are a range of abstract formats specific to each conference with guidelines usually provided through the conference website. This is an important point of reference for all potential presenters regarding abstract format, length and other specific requirements. In addition to requiring some form of abstract, conferences may also provide the opportunity for extended abstracts or short articles to be submitted. These are usually published separately within special issues or supplements of appropriate journals. Either way, presenting an abstract is usually a precursor to the authors writing a full journal article after having gained valuable feedback from the conference delegates.

1.3 Using abstracts

Many first-year university students are most likely not to have come into contact with abstracts prior to their degree studies. Indeed, Hartley (2004) notes that undergraduate students simply do not have the same experience of reading journal articles that researchers, academics and postgraduate students have acquired. Therefore it is likely to take undergraduates much longer to appreciate the key information presented within an abstract. Consequently, before getting to grips with writing abstracts it is important to first become accustomed to both searching for and reading abstracts as well as assessing the information contained within them. This approach will hopefully get you accustomed to the level of information presented in an abstract prior to writing one.

1.3.1 Searching for literature and extracting information

The tutors on your research methods modules have probably told you about the different ways to search for literature. Search engines such as Medline, Sports Discuss and Google Scholar, to name but a few, are all useful for finding academic information and journal articles. For the first exercise in this chapter log on to your recommended/preferred academic search engine. Search for journal articles in an area of your choice or the area of interest for the specific laboratory report that you are working on. At this stage you may want to refer to the 'Introduction and Literature Review' chapter where literature searching is covered in greater detail (see Section 2.3). If you have already undertaken this process please move on to Exercise 1.1.

Many academic and non-academic search engines will readily provide the abstract of your chosen articles. Indeed, in many instances this may be all the information that is required. For example, you may just want to give an example of an athletes' maximal oxygen uptake ($\dot{V}O_{2max}$), an example of how personality has been measured or the differences in performance time after a nutritional intervention. This is fine but remember that after reading the abstract you should always read the full article (Foote, 2006a, 2009a) to ensure that you fully appreciate the design and content of the research undertaken. Reading the full article will mean that you are more likely to gain more information about the study and your particular area of research. When referencing your sources some universities request that you specifically state when only the abstract has been used.

Exercise 1.1: Extracting information from an abstract

Choose one of the abstracts you have found in your literature search and use the IMRAD principle to determine the key aspects of the study. Read the abstract you have obtained and complete Table 1.1. Each abstract should include information relating to each of the headings provided so you should be able to pick out the key points of the study quite easily. If you have obtained a structured abstract this process should be more straightforward.

Table 1.1 Key points derived from each section of an abstract

Abstract component	Key point
Introduction/aims	
Participants	
Method	
Results	
Discussion/conclusion	

1.4 Writing an abstract

Although abstracts are generally a short summary of your project don't be mistaken into thinking that they will not take you a significant amount of time to write. Writing an abstract can be difficult, especially if you have a lot that you want to say but not many words to say it in. Writing concisely and informatively within a constrained word limit is often much more difficult than using a large number of words. It is therefore good practice to learn to write concisely. Unfortunately this is not a skill that many researchers or students initially hold and it does take practice. However, writing does improve with experience. For many undergraduate students the abstract is written quickly as an afterthought, usually just before binding and submitting the final version of their dissertation. When writing your abstract always bear in mind how informative *you* expect abstracts to be when searching the literature and remember that this will be the first section seen by your assessor or reviewer!

1.4.1 Background to writing an abstract

Writing an abstract means to extract and summarise (Alexandrov and Hennerici, 2007). A number of researchers concerned with educational and scientific writing have examined the effectiveness of (structured) abstracts for the reader as well as providing advice and guidance for writing them (Hartley, 2000, 2004; Squires, 1990). However, these points are just as important for non-structured abstracts, as well as for writing in general, so are worthy of note here. You may also want to refer to the section on 'General Writing Tips' later in this text (see Section 6.3).

   Hartley (2000) noted that there are three important aspects to consider when assessing the clarity of structured abstracts: the language or readability of the abstract, the sequence of information or structure of the abstract and the typography or presentation. When considering the first point, avoid the use of complex terminology or jargon for key concepts so that they can be understood by readers who are not subject experts (Hartley, 2000). You should also write in the past tense. The second point relates to providing a logical flow of information within the text and is consistent with the IMRAD principle (Alexandrov and Hennerici, 2007; Hartley, 2000; Pamir, 2002). The third point is concerned with the format of your abstract, and is therefore of most interest to journal editors. Table 1.2 considers in more detail the content that should be contained within each part of an abstract. After consulting Table 1.2 complete Exercise 1.2 to help you to appreciate how to get the key points of your study across succinctly. As abstracts are not usually expected in a laboratory report this exercise is more suited towards students writing up their final-year projects who have a sizeable data set to analyse and report.

Table 1.2 Key components of abstracts and what should be contained in each one

Title – Clear and concise, but not too short as to leave the reader uninformed.
The opening statement – there does not have to be a lengthy introduction or justification for the study, often the aims will suffice.

Participants – give as much details as you can regarding your participants. This information is usually presented in one or two sentences and is often accompanied by a statement regarding ethics committee approval – although this is more likely to be reserved for the method section within the report.

Method – the reader must get a good idea of what you have done. For the specific points regarding exercise protocols or measurements, for example, the reader can refer to the method section in the full article. If the research was concerned with a validation or new exercise protocol there may be a bias towards this aspect in the abstract.

Results – this is one of the most important aspects of the abstract as readers will want to know what has been found. Pick out the most important findings which relate to your research question or hypothesis. If the word limit allows, add appropriate values. Any abbreviations used should be defined in the previous methods section.

Conclusions – you will note that we haven't considered a discussion component. This is mainly due to the fact that there are not enough words available to provide a full discussion of the results, therefore the conclusion is used to present the key findings. You need to ensure that your conclusion is consistent with the key results reported earlier and the aims of your study.

Exercise 1.2: Writing an abstract

For the data you have collected in your project or one of the data sets provided in Appendix 1 try the following exercises.

Exercise 1.2a

With reference to Tables 1.1 and 1.2 write a summary of your research in approximately 400 words. You may find it useful to first consult Table 1.2 and then complete Table 1.1 which we used in Exercise 1.1 to determine the key information in a given abstract, but this time you are writing *your* abstract and need to ensure that you provide what *you* think is important.

Exercise 1.2b

Once you have completed Exercise 1.2a, try to reduce the length of your abstract to approximately 200 words.

To help you, an example of a longer abstract such as for a dissertation and a shorter abstract such as for a journal article have been provided (see Example abstract 1 and 2).

Example abstract 1: Maximal oxygen uptake lab, approximately 400 words

Assessment of maximal oxygen uptake during running, cycling and arm cranking

The aim of this study was to determine the maximal oxygen uptake during running, cycling and arm cranking. Ten healthy none specifically trained males (age 19 (2.6) years; height, 1.79 (6.7) m, body mass, 71.2 (7.1) kg) volunteered to participate in this study which had received University Ethics Committee approval. Participants undertook three incremental exercise tests to volitional exhaustion in order to determine maximal oxygen uptake ($\dot{V}O_{2max}$). The protocols were undertaken either during treadmill running (TR; Powerjog), cycle ergometry (CE; Monark 813E) and arm crank ergometry (ACE; Lode). The TR protocol involved an initial speed of 8 km.h^{-1} with increases in 2 km.h^{-1} every three minutes at a gradient of 1%. The CE protocol involved an initial power output of 70 W with further increases in power output of 35 W every three minutes whereas the ACE protocol involved an initial power output of 50 W and increases of 20 W every 2 min. Both CE and ACE were undertaken at 70 rev.min^{-1}. Expired gas samples were taken during the final minute of exercise. Heart rate was continually monitored throughout all tests. Ratings of perceived exertion (RPE) for cardiovascular strain were recorded in the last 15 s of each exercise stage. One way analysis of variance (ANOVA) demonstrated a significant difference between protocols ($P < 0.05$). Tukey post hoc analysis indicated that the $\dot{V}O_{2max}$ during TR (58.5 ± 6.1 ml.kg^{-1}min^{-1}) was similar to that achieved during CE (53.4 ± 5.4 ml.kg^{-1}min^{-1}; $P > 0.05$). During the ACE protocol participants obtained peak rather than maximal oxygen uptake ($\dot{V}O_{2peak}$) values with the mean $\dot{V}O_{2peak}$ being lowest during this mode of exercise than for TR and CE (38.7 ± 6.4 ml.kg^{-1}min^{-1}; $P > 0.05$). Maximal heart rates were similar during TR and CE (194 ± 5, 186 ± 5 beats.min^{-1}, respectively) but not different between exercise modes ($P > 0.05$). Peak heart rate during ACE was lower than for both TR and CE (179 ± 6 beats.min^{-1}; $P < 0.05$). RPE at volitional exhaustion followed a similar pattern to heart rate with lower values during ACE than for TR and CE (17.6 ± 2.3, 20.0 ± 1.2 and 18.8 ± 2.7, respectively; $P < 0.05$). The results of this study demonstrate that arm crank ergometry elicits lower peak oxygen uptake, heart rate and RPE than for treadmill running and cycle ergometry. The lower values for ACE are likely due to development of peripheral fatigue rather than to cardiorespiratory fatigue.

Word count: 386

Example abstract 2: Maximal oxygen uptake lab, approximately 200 words

Assessment of maximal oxygen uptake during running, cycling and arm cranking

The aim of this study was to determine maximal oxygen uptake during treadmill running (TR), cycle ergometry (CE) and arm crank ergometry (ACE). Ten healthy none specifically trained males volunteered to participate in this study which had received University Ethics Committee approval. Participants undertook three incremental exercise tests to volitional exhaustion in order to determine maximal oxygen uptake ($\dot{V}O_{2max}$). Expired gas samples were taken during the final exercise stage of each protocol. Heart rate and ratings of perceived exertion (RPE) were recorded in the last 15 s of each exercise stage. The $\dot{V}O_{2max}$ during TR (58.5 $\pm$ 6.1 ml.kg^{-1}min^{-1}) was similar to that achieved during CE (53.4 $\pm$ 5.4 ml.kg^{-1}min^{-1}; $P > 0.05$) with both being greater than for ACE (38.7 $\pm$ 6.4 ml.kg^{-1}min^{-1}; $P > 0.05$). Maximal heart rates were also similar during TR and CE (194 $\pm$ 5, 186 $\pm$ 5 beats.min^{-1}, respectively) with both being greater than for ACE ($P < 0.05$). RPE was lowest during ACE ($P < 0.05$). The results of this study demonstrate that arm crank ergometry elicits lower peak oxygen uptake, heart rate and RPE than for treadmill running and cycle ergometry. The lower values for ACE are likely due to development of peripheral fatigue rather than to cardiorespiratory fatigue.

Word count: 195

You can see from the example abstracts provided that there is a considerable amount of information presented in less than 400 words. Consider each aspect of Table 1.1 in conjunction with the example abstracts and use them to guide your writing and assess whether you have included enough information in your own abstracts. Can you get a good idea of what was done in the study and what was found? Figures 1.1 and 1.2 may help you decide.

Although many dissertation abstracts are not required to be as short as the 200 words suggested in Exercise 1.2b, some journal articles are. The exercise just completed will help you to appreciate writing concisely and reduce your word use. If you found this difficult, consider what your research question or research hypotheses were and your main findings. This is essentially what was in Table 1.1. These are the questions you were trying to answer and the information you were trying to find out. You may also find it helpful to try the exercise in reverse by first writing out your key findings in around 100 words and then gradually increasing your word count up to 200 or 400 words as required. Ensure that you include the important aspects suggested in Table 1.1.

Example abstract 1: Maximal oxygen uptake lab, approximately 400 words

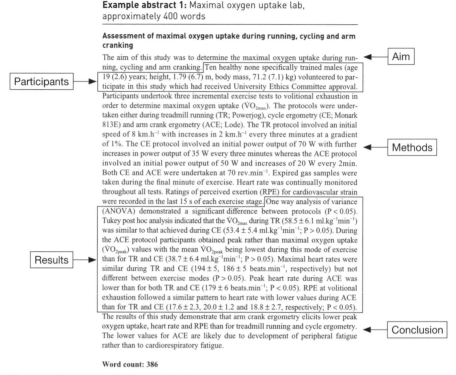

Assessment of maximal oxygen uptake during running, cycling and arm cranking

The aim of this study was to determine the maximal oxygen uptake during running, cycling and arm cranking. Ten healthy none specifically trained males (age 19 (2.6) years; height, 1.79 (6.7) m, body mass, 71.2 (7.1) kg) volunteered to participate in this study which had received University Ethics Committee approval. Participants undertook three incremental exercise tests to volitional exhaustion in order to determine maximal oxygen uptake ($\dot{V}O_{2max}$). The protocols were undertaken either during treadmill running (TR; Powerjog), cycle ergometry (CE; Monark 813E) and arm crank ergometry (ACE; Lode). The TR protocol involved an initial speed of 8 km.h^{-1} with increases in 2 km.h^{-1} every three minutes at a gradient of 1%. The CE protocol involved an initial power output of 70 W with further increases in power output of 35 W every three minutes whereas the ACE protocol involved an initial power output of 50 W and increases of 20 W every 2min. Both CE and ACE were undertaken at 70 rev.min^{-1}. Expired gas samples were taken during the final minute of exercise. Heart rate was continually monitored throughout all tests. Ratings of perceived exertion (RPE) for cardiovascular strain were recorded in the last 15 s of each exercise stage. One way analysis of variance (ANOVA) demonstrated a significant difference between protocols (P < 0.05). Tukey post hoc analysis indicated that the $\dot{V}O_{2max}$ during TR (58.5 ± 6.1 ml.kg^{-1}min^{-1}) was similar to that achieved during CE (53.4 ± 5.4 ml.kg^{-1}min^{-1}; P > 0.05). During the ACE protocol participants obtained peak rather than maximal oxygen uptake ($\dot{V}O_{2peak}$) values with the mean $\dot{V}O_{2peak}$ being lowest during this mode of exercise than for TR and CE (38.7 ± 6.4 ml.kg^{-1}min^{-1}; P > 0.05). Maximal heart rates were similar during TR and CE (194 ± 5, 186 ± 5 beats.min^{-1}, respectively) but not different between exercise modes (P > 0.05). Peak heart rate during ACE was lower than for both TR and CE (179 ± 6 beats.min^{-1}; P < 0.05). RPE at volitional exhaustion followed a similar pattern to heart rate with lower values during ACE than for TR and CE (17.6 ± 2.3, 20.0 ± 1.2 and 18.8 ± 2.7, respectively; P < 0.05). The results of this study demonstrate that arm crank ergometry elicits lower peak oxygen uptake, heart rate and RPE than for treadmill running and cycle ergometry. The lower values for ACE are likely due to development of peripheral fatigue rather than to cardiorespiratory fatigue.

Aim
Participants
Methods
Results
Conclusion

Word count: 386

Figure 1.1 Annotated abstract for Exercise 1.2a

Example abstract 2: Maximal oxygen uptake lab, approximately 200 words

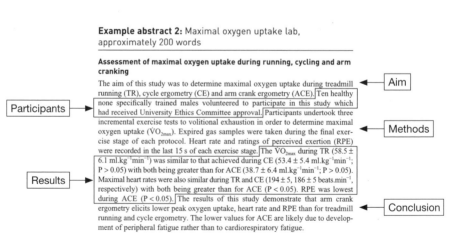

Assessment of maximal oxygen uptake during running, cycling and arm cranking

The aim of this study was to determine maximal oxygen uptake during treadmill running (TR), cycle ergometry (CE) and arm crank ergometry (ACE). Ten healthy none specifically trained males volunteered to participate in this study which had received University Ethics Committee approval. Participants undertook three incremental exercise tests to volitional exhaustion in order to determine maximal oxygen uptake ($\dot{V}O_{2max}$). Expired gas samples were taken during the final exercise stage of each protocol. Heart rate and ratings of perceived exertion (RPE) were recorded in the last 15 s of each exercise stage. The $\dot{V}O_{2max}$ during TR (58.5 ± 6.1 ml.kg^{-1}min^{-1}) was similar to that achieved during CE (53.4 ± 5.4 ml.kg^{-1}min^{-1}; P > 0.05) with both being greater than for ACE (38.7 ± 6.4 ml.kg^{-1}min^{-1}; P > 0.05). Maximal heart rates were also similar during TR and CE (194 ± 5, 186 ± 5 beats.min^{-1}, respectively) with both being greater than for ACE (P < 0.05). RPE was lowest during ACE (P < 0.05). The results of this study demonstrate that arm crank ergometry elicits lower peak oxygen uptake, heart rate and RPE than for treadmill running and cycle ergometry. The lower values for ACE are likely due to development of peripheral fatigue rather than to cardiorespiratory fatigue.

Aim
Participants
Methods
Results
Conclusion

Word count: 195

Figure 1.2 Annotated abstract for Exercise 1.2b

1.5 Critiquing an abstract and common errors

When asked to undertake a critique of a piece of work or a scientific study, most students focus upon negative aspects. Indeed, from an assessors' perspective these are often the key points that are immediately obvious and likely to be commented upon. However, noting positive aspects, which may not be explicitly obvious, is just as important (see Chapter 2, Section 2.8). To demonstrate some common errors that students regularly exhibit when writing abstracts, and to make you aware of some key aspects to avoid, an example of a poorly written abstract is provided in Exercise 1.3.

Exercise 1.3: Critiquing an abstract

Read the abstract and use Table 1.3 to note how many errors you can spot or improvements that could be made. Try to find ten. However, there are at least 15 more immediate points to consider (see Table 1.4), but there may be more! Within your critique you should always consider the required word length and the information required from each section of the study.

Example abstract 3

Title – Lab report

$\dot{V}O_{2max}$ is really important. It is the most important factor to show fitness levels in different people. We tested ten students to see if there was a difference in their values. Treadmill testing gave the largest values (58.417) and arm exercise the lowest. Exercise on the bike was a greater value than arm cranking. The $\dot{V}O_{2max}$ values for the three tests were different (58.417, 53, 38.7 ± 6.4 ml.kg^{-1}min^{-1}). Heart rate (194.12 bpm, 186, 178.7) was recorded in the last seconds of the exercise stage whereas Douglas bags were recorded at the end of each test. Our results show that treadmill testing is best.

Table 1.3 Points to improve/abstract errors

1.	....
2.	....
3.	....
4.	....
5.	....
6.	....
7.	....
8.	....
9.	....
10.	....

Table 1.4 Potential errors within example abstract 3

1. Title does not inform the reader of what was done. Each lab that you undertake will have aims or a specific title.
2. $\dot{V}O_{2max}$ is not defined and no subscript is used.
3. Third-person past tense not used.
4. No participant characteristics provided.
5. No indication of the protocols used prior to results.
6. No units for values provided.
7. Too many decimal places for variables presented.
8. Inconsistent decimal places given.
9. Terminology of 'bike' incorrect, should read 'cycle ergometer'.
10. Timing of heart rate measures and Douglas bag collections (method) given after some results already stated.
11. Decimal values used for heart rates, units wrong and not reported correctly.
12. States values were different but there is no indication of tests used or P values, or the direction of any differences.
13. Awkward wording throughout.
14. Abstract very short and not informative.
15. Concluding statement – why is treadmill testing best, and what is meant by this?

1.6 Chapter summary and reflection

This chapter has provided an overview of different types of abstracts and how you may extract information from them. We also considered how to plan and write an abstract using the same tools as for extracting information from them. This means that when you are writing your abstract you will hopefully include what you consider to be important for the reader to know. You will also find the chapters of this text relating to the methods and results sections of dissertations helpful in reporting the key aspects required for your abstract. To assess your understanding of abstracts answer the following questions:

- What is an abstract?
- What different types of abstract are there?
- What information is contained within an abstract?
- How should you approach writing an abstract?
- What are the common errors when writing abstracts?

1.7 Further activities

Go to the website of a journal that you regularly read or are aware of. Find the author guidelines and consider the advice given for writing and presenting abstracts.

Consult the methods and results chapters of this text to provide guidance in reporting key aspects of these sections of a dissertation within your abstract (see Chapters 3 and 4).

If you are submitting a conference abstract consult the conference website for example abstracts or look at journals where special editions have published previous abstracts for that conference.

Chapter 2

Introductions and literature reviews

In this chapter you will be able to:

- appreciate the role of an introduction (Section 2.1)
- differentiate between an introduction and a literature review (Section 2.2)
- undertake a literature search (Section 2.3)
- extract and use information from literature sources (Section 2.4)
- practice writing an introduction (Section 2.5)
- critique an introduction (Section 2.6)
- plan and write a literature review (Section 2.7)
- critique a journal article (Section 2.8)
- develop your aims, objectives and hypotheses (Section 2.9)
- identify common problems when writing introductions (Section 2.10)

2.1 An introduction to introductions

All types of scientific report will have some form of introductory section. Although the structure and length of these may differ the function of introductions is essentially the same: to move the reader from what is known about an area to what is unknown or to move the reader from general to specific information (Foote, 2006b). For a dissertation or scientific journal articles the introduction will end with the research question and hypothesis, whereas for an undergraduate lab report it is likely to end with the aims and objectives of the specific lab class.

Foote (2006a) considers a scientific article's introduction to be as important as the need to make a good impression in a job application. Indeed, imagine reading an introduction to a journal article or lab report where the author does not clearly present the information or effectively develop their experimental aims and objectives. Would you continue reading or give the report many marks? The following sections will consider how an introduction may differ between lab reports and dissertations as well as how your introduction may be integrated within a literature review.

2.1.1 Introductions in lab reports and journal articles

Depending on your level of study the introduction to your lab report will serve a number of purposes. However, all introductions require you to have read widely and to have reviewed the literature to some extent. The exercise accompanying this section will help you determine the type of information usually included within an introduction.

At the simplest level the introduction, as the name of the section implies, should *introduce* any key terms or concepts. For example, consider a first-year lab report relating the measurement of energy expenditure at rest and during exercise, probably using techniques for the first time. Here the reader, and certainly the assessor, will be expecting to see evidence of understanding and background reading rather than the development of a rationale for a Nobel-prize-winning research study. This is because undergraduate lab classes are generally designed to teach the skills and processes required for both your final-year project and professional career. It is your final-year project which is most likely to have a novel research aspect to it.

Introductions usually start with a more general or 'introductory' paragraph and become more specific as the introduction develops, culminating in the aims of your study (see Figure 2.1). Continuing with our energy expenditure example the introduction could take the form outlined in Figure 2.2. (It is important to note that the content of your introduction will clearly depend upon the contents and aims of the specific lab class. The following example is used purely to demonstrate a point.) Depending on the specific content required the flow chart in Figure 2.2 could demonstrate a general understanding of what energy expenditure is, how it can be measured (reflecting the methods used in the lab class) and what you would expect to find. From this the reader will hopefully be aware of whether the student understands the key concepts required. As the introduction progresses more specific details emerge relating to the specific activities undertaken within the lab class. These activities will be reflected in your aims and objectives (see Section 2.9). It is important to note that you should always follow the assessment guidelines provided by your tutor regarding the required content. Also consider the word count if one is stipulated. Whether you have been given specific guidelines or not you need to spend time planning the content of your introduction to reflect the aims of the class. If you are struggling to come up with key aspects of your lab report to include in the introduction you should consider the keywords contained within the title of your lab report, the aims or objectives and the key procedures undertaken in the methods.

As your lab classes become more complex throughout your degree studies, and certainly when writing journal articles, the introduction is used to serve the purpose of justification (Hopkins *et al.*, 2009). This is generally required to justify your research

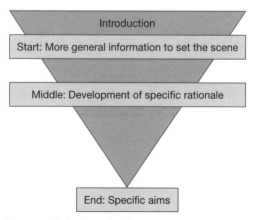

Figure 2.1 General format of the introduction

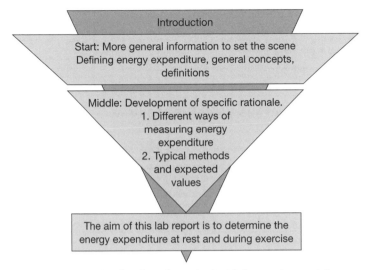

Figure 2.2 Example introduction for a hypothetical lab report examining energy expenditure

question or, as it is often termed, 'generate the rationale' for your study. For example, you may need to justify the use of a particular group of participants or research design (Hopkins *et al.*, 2009). The information you present should convince the reader that you have a sound reason for the study being undertaken. Whether you are writing an undergraduate lab report or writing up your fiftieth research paper all introductions must reflect the scientific question being asked and therefore what has been done within the study. A common error in lab report introductions is going 'off topic' – presenting what may be correct but irrelevant information. Although Exercise 2.1 focuses on journal articles, and the introductions to these differ from those of lab reports, the exercise is designed to help you consider the flow of information presented.

Exercise 2.1: What is in an introduction?

Choose a journal article relating to the area of your lab report or project. Make sure that it is a study which has collected some original data. Read the introduction and for each paragraph make a short note (one or two words only) of the key point that is being made or what aspect is being described. This approach could also be used when you are planning or proofreading your work.

Paragraph 1: ....

Paragraph 2: ....

Paragraph 3: ....

Paragraph 4: ....

Ask yourself the following questions:

1. Is there a logical flow of information?
2. How do the key points you have noted above compare to the title of the article and the aims?

Also consider the point made earlier regarding the development of the rationale:

3. Why is it important to have done this study?
4. What did you know beforehand?
5. What is the new aspect to be investigated?

2.2 Introduction versus literature review

One important question often asked by final-year project students is 'what is the difference between an introduction and a literature review?'. The answer relates to the type of the report you are writing. For shorter reports, such as undergraduate lab reports and scientific research studies, the introduction is as considered above: a short informative introduction to the area to establish your area of study or the research question. If you look at any published journal articles you should be able to see this (see Exercise 2.1). Although your introduction will contain references to previous research and briefly review the area, a 'literature review' per se is generally a much longer chapter within a thesis such as those written by final-year undergraduate and postgraduate students. Here the examiner is looking to establish that the student has a greater breadth and depth of knowledge, that there is a clear understanding of the chosen topic area and that the current, pertinent literature has been surveyed. For this reason undergraduate and postgraduate dissertations generally have both an introduction and a literature review, whereas lab reports only have an introduction. In final-year or postgraduate dissertations the introduction sets the scene for the study by giving an overview of the main topic of the thesis in two or three pages. The introduction would then be followed by the main literature review to provide a broader, in-depth review of pertinent literature. Figure 2.1 can now be expanded to demonstrate these differences (see Figure 2.3).

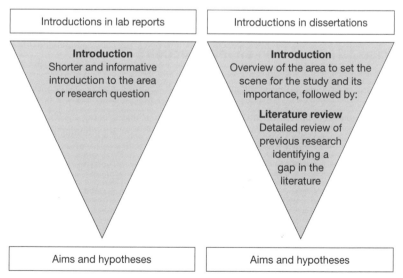

Figure 2.3 Introductions in lab reports and dissertations

2.2.1 Types of literature review

Within your literature search you will come across both original research articles and review articles. The latter are an ideal way to introduce yourself to a topic and also to see how literature reviews are structured. Literature reviews consist of a detailed and comprehensive narrative analysis of recent or evolving developments in specific topics (Ng and Peh, 2010a). Literature reviews may also help to consolidate data or opinions within a specific area or re-evaluate current knowledge in light of new findings or concepts. In this respect, literature reviews are often more up to date than textbooks (Green *et al.*, 2001). Although review articles may synthesise information from previous studies they generally do not present new data. This is the main difference between 'original' journal articles and literature reviews. The former have methods and results sections whereas the latter do not. For undergraduate and postgraduate students your literature review needs to demonstrate that you understand the area and current theories as well as the underlying processes or mechanisms. Furthermore, and importantly, you also need to identify a gap (or gaps) in the literature which can then be developed into your research question and subsequently your aims and hypotheses.

Literature reviews can be further separated into 'systematic' and 'narrative' reviews. The latter are sometimes termed 'non-systematic reviews', although this does not mean that a systematic approach has not been undertaken or that they are any less worthy (Sandelowski, 2008). Within both the scientific and educational literature there are a range of articles providing guidance on how to approach writing both narrative (Green *et al.*, 2001; Peh and Ng, 2010) and systematic (Ng and Peh, 2010a; Sandelowski, 2008; Wieseler and McGauran, 2010) reviews of literature, and on how to search scientific literature (Foote, 2009a). The purpose of this section is to provide an awareness of the different types of literature review and reviewing processes. As noted earlier, regardless of whether you are writing an introduction for a lab report or an article for a journal, a literature review is essential.

2.2.1.i Systematic literature reviews

Systematic literature reviews are often found in medical or clinical areas of research and are considered to be the cornerstone of evidence-based practice (Sandelowski, 2008). Such reviews help clinicians keep up to date with medical research findings and aid in the development of practical guidelines and policy decision making (Weiseler and McGauran, 2010). As the approach undertaken when writing systematic reviews is explicitly structured this process is considered to be the least biased and most rational way to search and report literature (Ng and Peh, 2010b). So how does a systematic review differ from other reviews? The key factor is the way in which the research studies are searched and subsequently included within or excluded from the review. For example, systematic reviews often relate to clinical trials where patient populations, age ranges, types of drugs or interventions employed, randomised control trials, double blind studies, etc. may all differ and significantly affect any clinical outcome. Ng and Peh (2010b) give the example of a literature search where 121 articles were retrieved from a given database. Fifty-one of these articles were excluded after reading the abstract. Of the 70 remaining articles, 42 were excluded as they did not fit the criteria for the review, leaving 28 articles to be included.

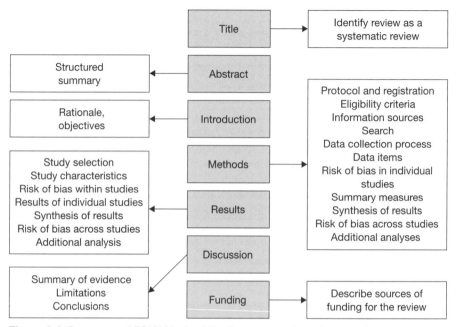

Figure 2.4 Summary of PRISMA checklist for systematic reviews and meta-analyses
Source: based on Moher *et al.* (2009)

Owing to the importance of systematic reviews in shaping clinical practice, and in order to provide consistency in systematic reviewing, the 'Preferred Reporting Items for Systematic Reviews and Meta-Analyses' (PRISMA) statement was developed. The PRISMA statement provides a 27-item checklist for systematic reviews and is available online (www.prisma-statement.org) as well as being published through a number of journals such as the *British Medical Journal* (e.g. Moher *et al.*, 2009). Many of the key components to be included in systematic reviews represent the range of possible subheadings included within structured abstracts (see Chapter 1, Section 1.2.1). Although this structured approach requires (and hopefully ensures) all key aspects of importance to clinicians and specific clinical outcomes are included, many of these factors are not key components for Sport and Exercise Science, which generally involves 'healthy' or non-clinical participants. However, the underlying principles for searching literature are essentially the same as for narrative reviews and it is certainly worth looking at the components of the PRISMA statement. A summary of the items presented in the PRISMA statement are shown in Figure 2.4. These will be considered later in this chapter (See Section 2.3 on literature searching). For details regarding the specific content of the PRISMA statement please consult the full document.

2.2.1.ii Narrative literature reviews

Narrative literature reviews are the most commonly found form of literature review in Sport and Exercise Science. However, like systematic reviews, narrative reviews often provide a statement regarding the search terms used and any inclusion or exclusion criteria applied to the various research studies obtained. In contrast to systematic reviews no relevant report is excluded (Sandelowski, 2008) and authors must be careful to avoid bias and remain objective in their information extraction (Green *et al.*, 2001). Narrative reviews therefore have the potential to be more wider reaching and inclusive than systematic reviews. However, regardless of whether you are writing a systematic or narrative review you first have to acquire your literature sources. Therefore, we will next address the basics of searching literature.

2.3 Literature searching

Your initial literature search will depend upon how familiar or experienced you are with a topic (Thomas and Nelson, 2001) and your current level of understanding of the area. Students who are not well grounded in a topic may benefit from reading appropriate textbooks and other sources of information (Thomas and Nelson, 2001). This approach is the most likely starting point for most undergraduate students, especially in their first year of study. For those students who are more confident in their understanding of their topic area reading a review article is a good first step. Not only will review articles provide up-to-date information at the time of publication, they will also give an overview of the area and recommendations for future research. In addition there is likely to be a long list of references to consult.

Through university modules on research methods, most students will have been made aware of the range of literature search engines and how to use them. Tutorials relating to this will often be available through your university or college library or through the education sections of medical journals, for example Greenhalgh (1997). Scientific search engines are a great way to get an idea of what literature is available on your chosen topic but also, depending on your university or college library subscriptions, this is a good way of obtaining electronic copies of journals. When you first obtain an article in a literature search it is likely that you will be able to access the abstract. This will give you an overview of the study and the key findings (see Chapter 1). Although it is always best to read the full article the abstract may give you some important and useable information. However, your search doesn't have to be limited to electronic or web-based searches. Don't forget that browsing the hard copies of journals on library shelves and in their reference lists is also a good way of finding information.

When considering the process of searching the literature a number of important factors should be considered (Foote, 2009a; Figure 2.5). First, consider the basics of undertaking literature searches, including determining the search terms to be used, databases to be searched, range of dates to search, type of articles to consider, etc. Second, the output of the search should be reviewed. Your resultant output may require your search terms to be refined to enable a more helpful search output or a manageable number of sources to be obtained. The third consideration is then the 'explication', or analysing and explaining the literature in order to construct the review (Foote, 2009a). Thomas and Nelson (2001) suggest six steps to ensure a thorough and productive literature review. When combining these steps with Foote's considerations you can see that although experienced and less experienced researchers may have different starting points for their searches they still undertake essentially the same processes (Figure 2.6). As you progress through your project it is also very important to update your searches as new and pertinent literature may be published while you are writing

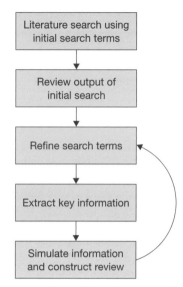

Figure 2.5 Schematic representation of literature searching and writing
Source: based on Foote (2009a)

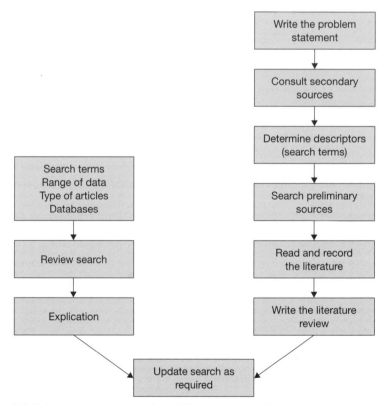

Figure 2.6 Schematic representation of literature searching
Sources: based on Foote (2009a) (left) and Thomas and Nelson (2001) (right)

up your project. As already noted, always read the full text of any article of interest and do not dismiss those articles that you can't get free online. Most universities have excellent inter-library loan systems and many also allow students of other universities to access to their resources. This aspect is certainly worth checking out.

Exercise 2.2: Literature searching

When searching for literature, note that if your search terms are quite general, such as 'anxiety', 'performance' or 'carbohydrate ingestion', you will have many thousands of results. You may find it easier to include more specific search terms such as the specific aspect of performance or sport you are interested in. Refining your search terms will provide a more specific and useable search output. Table 2.1 shows that although search results can initially be overwhelming they can then be constrained and reduced to those more appropriate to your needs. Searching for literature and getting to grips with appropriate search terms is a skill in itself. However, the more you search for information and the more you read around an area, the more likely you are going to be able to refine and undertake your searches successfully.

Within Table 2.1 are spaces for you to add your own search terms. Try different combinations of terms to obtain a useable output of potential articles. Once you have done this move on to the next section.

Table 2.1 Likely outputs from one search engine for three topics in Sport and Exercise Science

General search		
Area of interest	*Search terms*	*Number of articles found**
Anxiety	Anxiety	127 289
Performance	Performance	480 950
Carbohydrate ingestion	Carbohydrate ingestion	18 139
Your area of interest	....	....
Specific search		
Area of interest	*Search terms*	*Number of articles found*
Anxiety	Anxiety AND Tennis	21
Performance	Performance AND Running AND Elite	463
Carbohydrate ingestion	Carbohydrate ingestion AND Marathon running	24
Your area of interest	....	
	....	
	....	....

*From a typical scientific or academic search engine on any given date

2.4 Extracting information and using literature sources

Now that you have undertaken a literature search and obtained a range of information sources, what do you do with them? When you are using your various sources of information it is important to be able to extract exactly what you want from them. This may seem obvious, but when you haven't used this type of information before it may not be as straightforward as you think. Furthermore, it is likely that within your literature review or lab report introduction you will be explicitly required to use scientific literature to back up your statements.

So, what information is important? This will depend quite simply upon what you require. Your needs may be quite broad, such as an example of how anxiety is measured or an example of a personality questionnaire. Conversely, your needs may be more detailed, such as an in-depth explanation of the mechanisms of fatigue or how anxiety differs between performers. Review articles will often include a table that summarises key research studies. This is a very useful way to consolidate your thoughts on the available literature and consistently assess the same key points from each article you have read. Indeed, when you are reading journal articles certain aspects may continually come to mind that may affect the results of a given study. For example, the participants studied, the protocols or methods used and the design of the experiment as well as specific measures taken can all affect the results obtained. With this in mind, summary tables are likely to include information regarding participants and methodological aspects. Consider these aspects with respect to the key components of a structured abstract (as noted in Chapter 1) and for systematic reviews. When using a summary table the reader can quickly assess different approaches taken within the area and how diverse these may be, which may be why there are differing viewpoints within a topic.

Whether or not you include a summary table in your thesis is down to personal choice and supervisory guidance. However, as a way of summarising what may be quite a daunting pile of research papers a summary table can very useful. A simple approach to summarising data will relate to your research question. For example, if your research question relates to the effects, on performance of a nutritional supplement, such as sodium bicarbonate or creatine phosphate ingestion, what is the general consensus? Here you would simply need to note for each research study that you read whether performance was improved, negatively affected or not affected at all. You might then want to find out if there was a consistent aspect in those studies that found enhanced performance. Examining the participant characteristics, exercise protocols, administration of the supplement, etc. may help pinpoint specific important factors. Similarly, you may be interested in the effects of anxiety on performance. You could again determine from your research articles those that showed performance to be affected by anxiety and those that did not. From here you may be able to determine a certain level of anxiety where performance is affected or whether certain groups of participants or certain types of skill are most affected by anxiety. You could of course obtain all this information from simply reading the research articles and remembering the facts, but you may find that summarising your data this way is helpful.

Exercise 2.3 will help you to assess how well you extract information and also give you some practice in determining what may be important in a given source of information. When recording information from literature sources, Thomas and Nelson (2001) suggest considering, amongst other factors, the characteristics of participants, instruments and tests (including reliability and validity), testing procedures, treatments applied, study design, and statistical analysis and key findings. The list of factors that you may be interested in will be similar to those usually considered when critiquing studies (see Section 2.8). Indeed, there are a range of guidelines for critiquing scientific studies, such as a checklist sheet from Thomas and Nelson, the PRISMA statement, a peer-review checklist developed by Seals and Tanaka (2000) and an assessment checklist sheet for narrative reviews (Green *et al.*, 2001). However, as many of these are designed for the peer review of journal articles they are possibly more complicated and consider more factors than you require at present. Consider what it is you really want to find out from a particular source. You may not need all that detail.

Exercise 2.3: Extracting and using information

Following this exercise are four abstracts relating to the maximal oxygen uptake example lab class we are using within this book. The abstracts were obtained from a Medline (PubMed) literature search using the following search terms: 'Maximal oxygen uptake AND elite marathon runners'; 'Maximal oxygen uptake AND elite cyclists'; and 'peak oxygen uptake AND upper body exercise'. These are terms that you may use if interested in examining the aerobic capacity, fitness or physiological responses of athletes across exercise types. The abstracts give values or information relating to four different scenarios but can be combined quite fluently in a number of ways. These particular abstracts have been chosen simply because they provide information that can be used to help us demonstrate and practice the skill of extracting information, rather than for any other particular aspect. As with all sources it is up to you to critique them further and fully.

First make short notes on what you think the important findings are from each abstract. It is important to make notes in *your own words* rather than copying directly from the abstract or article. Once you have done this try and integrate the information you have highlighted. A worked example is also provided (see Table 2.2).

Table 2.2 Example key points from each abstract

Abstract 1	Maximal oxygen uptake increased with competition distance. Values for 800–1500-m athletes were 72.1 ml.kg^{-1}min^{-1} and for 5000–10,000-m group, 78.7 ml.kg^{-1}min^{-1}.
Abstract 2	Compared maximal physiological variables in men and women. Physiologically, triathletes were most like cyclists. Maximal oxygen uptake was greatest for the treadmill test, then cycling and then arm exercise.
Abstract 3	$\dot{V}O_{2max}$ of hockey players did not change during a competitive season, although values did tend to increase over the season. Body fat reduced during the season. Muscular strength reduced during the season.
Abstract 4	Peak oxygen uptake during arm exercise was greatest for able-bodied athletes when compared to wheelchair athletes. Peak oxygen uptake was lowest in a tetraplegic athlete when compared to paraplegic athletes.

Abstract 1: ....
....
....
....
....

Abstract 2: ....
....
....
....
....

Abstract 3: ....
....
....
....
....

Abstract 4: ....
....
....
....
....

Try and combine this information from each abstract into a summary sentence or paragraph. You may only be interested in one particular part of the abstract rather than the main results of the study, such as the $\dot{V}O_{2max}$ values for a group of athletes rather than their body temperature responses (e.g. Price and Campbell, 1999).

Summary: ....
....
....
....
....

How did you get on? It is important to note that there is no right or wrong answer to this activity as you will be presenting what *you* think is important. However, what you say or interpret has to be correct. The worked example following the abstracts shows a range of ways in which the information could be presented. This will differ depending on what you are trying to show.

Abstract 1

Svedenhag, J. and Sjödin, B. (1985) Maximal and submaximal oxygen uptakes and blood lactate levels in elite male middle- and long-distance runners. *International Journal of Sports Medicine* 5(5), 255–61 (reprinted by permission).

Physiological characteristics of elite runners from different racing events were studied. Twenty-seven middle- and long-distance runners and two 400-m runners belonging to the Swedish national team in track and field were divided, according to their distance preferences, into six groups from 400 m up to the marathon. The maximal oxygen uptake (VO2 max, ml $\times$ kg^{-1} $\times$ min^{-1}) on the treadmill was higher the longer the main distance except for the marathon runners (e.g., 800–1500-m group, 72.1; 5000–10,000-m group, 78.7 ml $\times$ kg^{-1} $\times$ min^{-1}). Running economy evaluated from oxygen uptake measurements at 15 km/h (VO$_2$ 15) and 20 km/h (VO2 20) did not differ significantly between the groups even though VO$_2$ 15 tended to be lower in the long-distance runners. The running velocity corresponding to a blood lactate concentration of 4 mmol/l (vHla 4.0) differed markedly between the groups with the highest value (5.61 m/s) in the 5000–10,000-m group. The oxygen uptake (VO2) at vHla 4.0 in percentage of VO2 max did not differ significantly between the groups. The blood lactate concentration after exhaustion (VO2 max test) was lower in the long-distance runners. In summary, the present study demonstrates differences in physiological characteristics of elite runners specializing in different racing events. The two single (but certainly inter-related) variables in which this was most clearly seen were the maximal oxygen uptake (ml $\times$ kg^{-1} $\times$ min^{-1}) and the running velocity corresponding to a blood lactate concentration of 4 mmol/l.

Abstract 2

O'Toole, M.L., Hiller, D.B., Crosby, L.O. and Douglas, P.S. (1987) The ultra-endurance triathlete: a physiological profile. *Medicine and Science in Sports and Exercise* **19**(1), 45–50.

To better characterize the athletes who participate in ultraendurance triathlons, 14 triathletes in training for the Hawaii IRONMAN triathlon were studied. A physical and physiological profile was developed from anthropometric measurements and oxygen uptake during maximal exercise on a treadmill, cycle ergometer, and arm ergometer. A comparison of the maximal values among exercise modes and between males and females was made. A comparison of height, weight, and percent body fat of these triathletes with elite athletes from the sports of swimming, cycling, and running showed the physique of triathletes to be most similar to that of cyclists. Oxygen uptake at maximal exercise was, for males and females, respectively: 68.8 ml $\times$ kg^{-1} $\times$ min^{-1}, 65.9 ml $\times$ kg^{-1} $\times$ min^{-1} on the treadmill; 66.7 ml $\times$ kg^{-1} $\times$ min^{-1}, 61.6 ml $\times$ kg^{-1} $\times$ min^{-1} on the cycle ergometer; and 49.1 ml $\times$ kg^{-1} $\times$ min^{-1}, 39.7 ml $\times$ kg^{-1} $\times$ min^{-1} on the arm ergometer. When comparing the highest oxygen uptake attained at maximal exercise in any one of the three exercise modes, the male triathletes are comparable to swimmers, but have a lower aerobic capacity than cyclists or distance runners. The female triathletes studied were able to attain oxygen uptake values greater than those previously reported for female athletes.

Abstract 3

Astorino, T.A., Tam, P.A., Rietschel, J.C., Johnson, S.M. and Freedman, T.P. (2004) Changes in physical fitness parameters during a competitive field hockey season. *Journal of Strength and Conditioning Research* **18**(4), 850–4.

Competitive field hockey requires a substantial amount of muscular strength, speed, and cardiovascular endurance. It is unknown how these parameters of physical fitness change between preseason conditioning to postseason recovery. Therefore, Division III female field hockey athletes (n = 13) completed tests of muscular strength, body composition, and maximal oxygen uptake (Vo(2)max) during each phase of their season. Muscular strength was assessed using 1 repetition maximum (RM) leg and bench press tests. Body composition was assessed by anthropometry (skinfolds [SKF]), circumferences ([CC]), and bioelectrical impedance analysis (BIA). Incremental treadmill testing was administered to assess Vo(2)max. Vo(2)max was unchanged during the season, although a trend ($p > 0.05$) was shown for a higher Vo(2)max during and after the season vs. before the season. Upper- (10%) and lower-body strength (14%) decreased ($p > 0.05$) during the season. Percent body fat (%BF) from BIA, fat mass (FM) from CC, and body mass index (BMI) were significantly lower ($p < 0.05$) in-season and postseason vs. preseason. In conclusion, preseason training was effective in decreasing %BF and increasing Vo(2)max, yet muscular strength was lost. Coaches should incorporate more rigorous in-season resistance training to prevent strength decrements. Moreover, these data support the superior levels of muscular strength and leanness in these athletes compared with age-matched peers.

Abstract 4

Price, M.J. and Campbell, I.G. (1999). Thermoregulatory responses of spinal cord injured and able-bodied athletes to prolonged upper body exercise and recovery. *Spinal Cord* **37**(11), 772–9. Reprinted by permission from Macmillan Publishers Ltd.

STUDY DESIGN: Single trial, two factor repeated measures design. SETTING: England, Cheshire. OBJECTIVES: To examine the thermoregulatory responses of able-bodied (AB) athletes, paraplegic (PA) athletes and a tetraplegic (TP) athlete at rest, during prolonged upper body exercise and recovery. METHODS: Exercise was performed on a Monark cycle ergometer (Ergomedic 814E) adapted for arm exercise at 60% VO2 peak for 60 min in cool conditions ('normal' lab temperature; 21.5+/−1.7 degrees C and 47+/−7.8% relative humidity). Aural and skin temperatures were continually monitored. RESULTS: Mean (+/−S.D.) peak oxygen uptake values were greater ($P < 0.05$) for the AB when compared to the PA (3.45+/−0.45 l min^{-1} and 2.00+/−0.46 l min^{-1}, respectively). Peak oxygen uptake for the TP was 0.91 l min^{-1}. At rest, aural temperature was similar between groups (36.2+/−0.3 degrees C, 36.3+/−0.3 degrees C and 36.3 degrees C for AB, PA and

TP athletes, respectively). During exercise, aural temperature demonstrated relatively steady state values increasing by 0.6+/−0.4 degrees C and 0.6+/−0.3 degrees C for the AB and PA athletes, respectively. The TP athlete demonstrated a gradual rise in aural temperature throughout the exercise period of 0.9 degrees C. Thigh skin temperature increased by 1.3+/−2.5 degrees C for the AB athletes (P < 0.05) whereas the PA athletes demonstrated little change in temperature (0.1+/−3.4 degrees C and −0.7 degrees C respectively). Calf temperature increased for the PA athletes by 1.0+/−3.6 degrees C (P < 0.05), whereas a decrease was observed for the AB athletes of −1.0+/−2.0 degrees C (P < 0.05) during the exercise period. During 30 min of passive recovery, the AB athletes demonstrated greater decreases in aural temperatures than those for the PA athletes (P < 0.05). Aural temperature for the TP increased peaking at 5 min of recovery remaining elevated until the end of the recovery period. Fluid consumption and weight losses were similar for the AB and PA athletes (598+/−433 ml and 403+/−368 ml; 0.38+/−0.39 kg and 0.38+/−0.31 kg, respectively), whereas changes in plasma volume were greater for the AB athletes (−9.8+/−5.8% and 4.36+/−4.9%, respectively; P < 0.05). CONCLUSION: The results of this study suggest that under the experimental conditions PA athletes are at no greater thermal risk than AB athletes. A relationship between the available muscle mass for heat production and sweating capacity appears evident for the maintenance of thermal balance. During recovery from exercise, decreases in aural temperature, skin temperature and heat storage were greatest for the AB athletes with the greatest capacity for heat loss and lowest for the TP athlete with the smallest capacity for heat loss. Initial observations on one TP athlete suggest substantial thermoregulatory differences when compared to AB and PA athletes.

Table 2.2 demonstrates some of the key information that could be taken from the abstracts provided. Please note that the importance of each key point will differ depending on what you are interested in reporting or stating. The examples below demonstrate some potential combinations of information. How you use the information will be determined by what you want to say in your introduction and the specific question that you are asking.

1. A general comment regarding measurement of maximal oxygen uptake:
   Maximal oxygen uptake values for a range of athletes have been determined (Astorino et al., 2004; O'Toole et al., 1987; Price and Campbell, 1999; Svedenhag and Sjödin, 1985).
2. Describing $\dot{V}O_{2max}$ within a specific athlete group:
   Svedenhag and Sjödin (1985) determined the maximal oxygen uptake of a range of elite runners. Athletes ranged from those competing at distances of 400 m up to the marathon. The greatest values were seen for 5000 to 10 000 m runners (78.7 ml.kg^{-1}min^{-1}).
3. Describing $\dot{V}O_{2max}$ across sports:
   Maximal oxygen uptake values are greatest in distance runners when compared to cyclists and wheelchair athletes (O'Toole et al., 1987; Price and Campbell, 1999; Svedenhag and Sjödin, 1985).

OR

Elite distance runners demonstrate $\dot{V}O_{2max}$ values of over 70 ml.kg^{-1}min^{-1} (Svedenhag and Sjödin, 1985). Triathletes have demonstrated lower $\dot{V}O_{2max}$ values than this during cycling (68.8 ml.kg^{-1}min^{-1}) and lower values still during arm exercise (49.1 ml.kg^{-1}min^{-1}; O'Toole *et al.*, 1987).

OR

$\dot{V}O_{2max}$ is generally greatest during treadmill running and cycling with lower values observed for arm exercise (O'Toole *et al.*, 1987; Price and Campbell, 1999; Svedenhag and Sjödin, 1985). Values may also change over a competitive season (Astorino *et al.*, 2004).

Now that you have practised extracting and linking information from different sources it is time to put your introduction together. The next section will help you do this.

2.5 Writing an introduction

Whether you are writing a lab report or dissertation, or are embarking upon writing a research paper or review article, you need to have a good grasp of what has been previously reported in the literature. Most authors addressing the different stages of a research project (Eston and Rowlands, 2000) or manuscript preparation (Altinörs, 2002) highlight the importance of undertaking an initial 'detailed survey' of the literature. Indeed, being well read in your area is an important first step of the writing process (Hall, 2011). Having read a wide range of pertinent literature you will then need to synthesise the information to develop and finalise your research question. For lab reports this will be more directed based upon what you have done in your classes, although it is still important to read widely.

When writing an introduction a number of authors suggest a 'three paragraph approach' (e.g. Alexandrov, 2004; Foote, 2006a). This follows the 'general to specific' nature of introductions noted earlier with the information presented leading clearly on to the aims and hypotheses. Consider the first exercise in this chapter where you described each paragraph of an introduction using one or two words. We will use this principle in writing an introduction (Exercise 2.4).

Exercise 2.4: Writing an introduction

For the key aspects of your introduction plan out three paragraphs (you can of course use more). Start by considering the key aspects you need to cover based on your title, the aims of the study and the methods undertaken in your class.

Paragraph 1: ....

Paragraph 2: ....

Paragraph 3: ....

Now expand each aspect using information from the literature to introduce each term, show how a term may be used or provide example values.

2.6 Critiquing an introduction

We noted earlier in the text (see Chapter 1) that when asked to critique a piece of writing it is important to note positive aspects as well as those that you consider could be improved. Being able to critique previous work is an important aspect of your research methods and scientific training and is considered in greater detail later in this chapter (Section 2.8). The skill of being able to critique your own work is of great importance and may help you to achieve better marks. Exercise 2.5 is designed to help you start critiquing introductions but you can also try it on your own work once you have prepared your first draft.

Exercise 2.5: Critiquing an introduction

In conjunction with Section 2.10 ('Common problems in writing introductions and literature reviews') read the example introduction provided and determine whether you think it would achieve many marks for a lab report assessment. Using the same skills that you used for critiquing abstracts in the previous chapter (Section 1.5, Exercise 1.3) note any good aspects or those that could be improved. Some useful comments are provided in Table 2.3.

Table 2.3 Points of critique for the example introduction

Overall the introduction is very short and does not provide information in a coherent way. There are also wording and referencing errors.

Paragraph 1
1. The paragraph refers to a previous study (Damavandi *et al.*, 2011) but it is incorrectly referenced and provides little if any information. It would be better to provide appropriate definitions of ground reaction forces and background information to start with.
2. The ground reaction force definitions are vague and incorrect and are also not referenced.
3. The third sentence is very general. It would be useful to start the introduction if it contained more information.
4. From the fourth sentence the introduction begins to provide methods information.

Paragraph 2
1. Some more background information is provided but it lacks specific details. The reader will be unable to determine specific facts from what is reported or why it is important to cite this study in relation to the lab report.
2. More definitions of ground reaction forces are given but these should really be in the first paragraph.
3. It is good that some applications of measuring ground reaction forces have been attempted. However, these are not referenced and the specific details relating to what measurements would be useful and how the results could be used is missing.

Paragraph 3
1. Both the aim and hypothesis are provided. However, the aim itself does not relate to what is covered in the introduction. It would be expected that if your aim relates to ground reaction forces in walking and running that these are described and explained in the introduction. Provide examples of expected values.
2. Likewise, the hypothesis does not provide an indication of which forces may be greatest.

Example introduction for ground reaction force lab report

Damavandi M looked at ground reaction forces in exercise (2011). Ground reaction forces are forces that the body produces during exercise. Biomechanics is therefore very important for sport and exercise science. In this lab class we will look at different ground reaction forces. We looked at different running speeds and measured the ground reaction forces with a force plate. The data was analysed.

Lipfert *et al.* (2011). Examined ground reaction forces and developed a model of ground reaction forces in running and walking. This is useful for assessing values when you can't measure them. Hall (1999) defines ground reaction forces in relation to Newton's third law of motion. These forces differ between people who are rearfoot and midfoot strikers. It is therefore important to measure these forces for footwear and injury concerns.

The aim of this lab class was to measure ground reaction forces in walking and running. We hypothesized that they would differ between conditions.

2.7 Planning and writing a literature review

There are a range of texts relating how to write literature reviews across a number of disciplines (e.g. Hart, 1998; Ridley, 2008). There are also some general texts within the area of Sport and Exercise Science regarding undertaking final-year projects (Lynch, 2010) and research methods (Thomas and Nelson, 2001) which contain useful information regarding literature searches and report writing. However, as writing a literature review is not the sole purpose of this book the aim of this section is simply to provide some basic guidance.

As noted earlier a literature review is a much more in-depth way of demonstrating your understanding of an area compared to a lab report introduction. In addition, it must form a solid basis for your research study and provide the rationale or justification for your study. By this we mean that you have to show that there is a gap in the literature which has not been examined and that this is what you intend to study. You need to make it clear why your study is different from those that have been reported previously. However, just because something has not been done before is not a good reason to study it! Thomas and Nelson (2001) consider type III and type IV errors. The former relates to asking the wrong research question and the latter relates to solving a problem that is not worth solving. A thorough literature review should hopefully prevent these errors occurring – along with the fifth error of researching something that has already been reported. For example, there have been many studies assessing differences in personality on exercise behaviours or whether carbohydrate ingestion improves performance, so why is your research study different to all the others? Ask yourself whether someone could read your literature review and, without reading your aims, have a good idea of what your research question is likely to be. If the answer is yes then you have done a good job. If it is likely that someone could read your literature review and be left struggling to see what you wish to examine then the review is not clear. Furthermore, if your aims do not relate to what you have reviewed then you are again off topic and you will need to refocus your review. By carefully planning your review in the same way as planning an introduction (see Exercises 2.3 to 2.5) each section of the review should be related to your research question.

Don't underestimate how difficult it may be to clearly justify your study. If you are struggling to get your ideas written down clearly try and explain your ideas to someone. Verbalising your thoughts may help focus your explanation. When my PhD supervisor was confronted with various unclear paragraphs of text he would ask me to simply tell him what I meant. When I did, in one or two sentences, he would then ask; 'Why didn't you just write that?' It may not be quite as easy as that all the time, and of course you will need to add your references and underlying theories or responses to explain your ideas, but it is certainly one method of clarifying your ideas. Many undergraduate and postgraduate supervisors, myself included, often repeatedly write questions or comments on students' work such as 'Why?' or 'How?' to get them to try and clarify and rationalise their research questions.

2.7.1 Planning a literature review

Before putting pen to paper you need to know the literature relating to your research questions – you also need to know your research question! Many students (especially undergraduate students) know this well before they may understand the specifics of the area being studied. Don't try and plan too much prior to reading the literature as you may find that your review plan changes dramatically as the story behind the underlying literature unfolds. Furthermore, literature reviews evolve as you undertake and write other sections of your project. This is also true when you are writing your discussion, as important components may come to light which you had not originally considered. You may then decide to add these areas to your review.

So, how do you start to plan your review? Consider the summary table you developed for your literature sources earlier in the chapter. From this you may find a pattern of responses or specific themes that you can use as subheadings (Hardy and Ramjeet, 2005). You will also need to critique the literature you have obtained. In addition, always have your research question in mind. Finally, ensure that you have read and summarised your research papers before attempting Exercise 2.6.

Do you remember the 'three paragraph approach' to writing introductions that we mentioned earlier? You may find it helpful to consider a similar approach to your literature review but this time, instead of three paragraphs, consider three sections (Figure 2.7). The first section should introduce the research area. Here, for example, you can state what areas the review will cover, if you undertook a systematic review

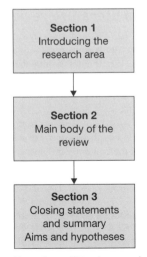

Figure 2.7 Three potential sections for a literature review

note what your search terms and criteria were (see Section 2.2.1.i), include why the area of study is important and list any potential applications for the results. It may also be useful to note the areas that you will be covering to give an overview of the reviews structure and content (Bem, 1995). If you always have your research hypotheses in mind this can give you significant direction in your planning.

The second section is the main body of the review. Unfortunately there is no easy answer as to how to plan this section as all reviews differ depending on what you are studying and what you intend to develop for your rationale. An important tip is not to try to cover everything but also not to limit yourself by only using one or two key references (especially if you only obtained recent electronic sources). In this section of your review a literature summary table can be very useful. Each factor that has emerged may help you devise the main headings and subheadings within the text. Here subheadings are essential so that the reader knows exactly what are they are supposed to be reading about. However, a common error here is when the text does not relate to the subheading. An error such as this can be overcome by careful proofreading and using the 'one word descriptors' for each of your paragraphs, as in Exercise 2.1, to ensure the content is relevant to the heading. An important point here is to note that for some research areas there may not be many articles relating to your research question. Students often struggle if there are no studies asking exactly the same research question that they have developed. This is not a problem – if there were similar studies why would yours be original? However, there will certainly always be a range of related studies from which you can develop your hypotheses. In addition, there are likely to be a number of key or opposing viewpoints on the subject area, and it is important to demonstrate that you know these and that you can back up and explain your decision.

The third and final section of the review should bring the review to a close, ending in a summary and your subsequent aims and hypotheses. Bem (1995) states that you should end a literature review with a bang rather than a whimper. What research has not been reported so far and which studies should be undertaken to bridge the gap in knowledge? Hopefully one of these suggestions will be related to your research hypothesis.

Exercise 2.6: Planning a literature review

Hopefully by now you will be happy with your research question and will be well read in the supporting literature. Consider the key themes within the literature and what factors have emerged as being important to the area. The suggestions in Section 1 and 3 below are simply to get you started in formulating or planning your review. For Section 2 revisit your literature summary table for key themes. Using these key themes is one approach that you may find useful. However, the content will vary with the area studied and your research question. Therefore, it is worth trying this approach even though you may use other methods to plan your literature review. You should always discuss the content with your supervisor.

Section 1

What areas will the review cover?
For systematic reviews, what search terms and criteria were considered?
Why is the area of study important?
What applications are there for the results of such studies?

Section 2

Consider the key themes as subheadings.

Section 3

What research has not been reported so far?
What studies should be undertaken to bridge the gap in knowledge?
Aims and objectives.
Hypotheses.

If you are struggling trying to plan your review, you may find it helpful to work backwards from your research question by considering what would be useful to discuss from specific to general points.

2.7.2 Writing a literature review

Once the key planning of your review has been done you can begin writing in earnest. At this stage you will have ideally read the literature, critiqued the studies and written or at least be happy with your research hypothesis. Essentially you will be adding detail to each of your subheadings. Note that your headings may well evolve as your writing does and your focus becomes clearer. Some headings may disappear and others may appear. Much of your writing will relate to the reporting and critiquing of research studies (see Section 2.8) and developing your research question so it is important that you are happy with extracting information from your literature sources (see Exercise 2.3). You must also ensure that you produce a clear overview. Reviews at undergraduate level often become either catalogues of information involving long lists of studies without any integration of key points or summaries of information with few links made between them. Try to avoid such an approach and make sure that you integrate your key studies together clearly and logically (see Exercise 2.3). If no one has reported an aspect of the area you are interested in it is perfectly acceptable to state that. However, in this instance you may have to think a little more laterally to try and develop aspects of your rationale.

Bem (1995) provides a helpful overview of scientific writing when considering literature reviews submitted to the journal *Psychological Bulletin*. Although literature review articles may differ from undergraduate and postgraduate dissertations the key aspects of scientific writing are essentially the same. Bem notes that a key factor differentiating between those articles accepted and rejected for publication is that of good writing and further notes that the primary criteria for good scientific writing are accuracy and clarity. For accuracy, ensure that any information provided is correct. Your supervisor is likely to know the details of many of the studies you are citing, and may well have written some of them, so they will know specific results and explanations. For clarity, make sure you state enough information to give an idea of the direction or magnitude or any previous results. For example, stating that 'ground reaction forces were different' is not very enlightening. Stating that 'ground reaction forces were greater during running than walking' or adding an idea of the size of such changes or absolute values provides a much clearer message to the reader. General writing tips are covered later in this text and it is recommended that you read that chapter while writing your review (see Chapter 6). The critique aspect of using literature is considered in Section 2.8.

2.8 Critiquing journal articles

The ability to think independently and critically is a key aspect of higher education (Ryall, 2010) and is particularly important in the final year of degree-level study. However, students often find critical analysis difficult. How do you go about beginning your critique of an article? How can you critique something that is already published? This section will hopefully provide answers to these common questions and give some ideas of how to approach the critical appraisal of a journal article or any other information source. Postgraduate students may find journal clubs or research seminar series quite useful for the discussion or critique of various journal articles or research studies, including their own.

What is critical analysis? Ryall (2010) notes that a critical thinker is able to make judgements based on sound reasoning. These judgements will depend on what is important to you and the sound reasoning is likely to relate to previous research findings and your interpretation of them. Young and Solomon (2009) state that critical analysis is a systematic approach used to determine the strengths and weaknesses of a journal article to assess both its usefulness and the validity of the reported findings. Greenhalgh (1997) states that critical analysis is the assessment of methodological quality. Importantly, Coughlan *et al.* (2007) note that critical analysis is not a criticism but an objective and balanced scrutiny of a piece of work, not only highlighting its strengths and weaknesses but to also ascertain whether the source is trustworthy and unbiased.

The majority of definitions of critical appraisal or critical thinking, such as those above, note that both the strengths and weaknesses of a source should be considered. Critique is not just pointing out negative or 'bad' points, it is also a consideration of what is new, novel and 'good'. Students can often be quite negative in critiquing work, but remember that if the research studies you read were truly 'bad' it is unlikely that they would have been published. Just because a study has not measured a variable that you are particularly interested in does not mean that it is bad, it probably just wasn't of key importance or interest to the authors. Furthermore, any criticism of other authors' work should be expressed in an objective manner (Wieseler and McGauran, 2010). Your critique should not be a demolition or 'trashing' of someone else's work (Ridley, 2008; Young and Solomon, 2009). Consider how you would react if similar comments were passed on your work.

So how do you go about critiquing a journal article? You have already done this at a basic level in extracting what you thought was important from the abstracts (see Exercise 2.4) and in establishing where gaps in the literature exist for your project area. Exercise 2.4 also noted that what you think is important may differ from what someone else considers to be important. Part of a critique is taking this one step further. Some authors suggest focussing upon the methods sections (Greenhalgh, 1997) and a lot of critique does indeed focus on the 'what did they do' aspects. Greenhalgh (1997) notes that most journal articles conform to the IMRaD principle, covering not only methods but the 'why did they do it?' (Introduction), 'What did they find?' (Results) and 'What do the results mean?' (Discussion) aspects. These other sections are also worthy of your critique.

2.8.1 Critical appraisal tools

There are a range of critical appraisal tools available in the literature which may help develop your critiquing skills. More seasoned academics are unlikely to use a structured profoma when critiquing or reviewing journal articles, instead relying predominantly upon their research and publishing experience. However, for less-experienced researchers published guidelines will be of much more value. Guidelines and advice have been produced for the critical appraisal of journal articles in both quantitative and qualitative research in nursing (Coughlan *et al.*, 1997; Ryan *et al.*, 2007), physiology (Seals and Tanaka, 2000), psychology (Hyman, 1995), medicine (Greenhalgh, 1997; Young and Solomon, 2009), general practice (MacAuley, 1994), public health (Heller *et al.*, 2008) and physical therapy (Domholdt *et al.*, 1994; Maher *et al.*, 2004). Although all these guides are very useful, they were developed for specific research disciplines – there is no 'gold standard' procedure. Therefore, whatever process is undertaken must evolve with advances in methodological and non-methodological factors (Greenhalgh, 1997). To illustrate this point, when you read older journal articles or 'classic' studies and critique them for not using a particular technique, bear in mind that many techniques commonly employed today may not have been widely available at the time of writing. Differences also exist between quantitative and qualitative research processes and in the way the critique process should be approached for both (Ryan *et al.*, 2007).

More general models of critical appraisal provide general concepts for the appraiser to consider. For example, Deane (2010) considers seven points for the general critique of information sources, including whether the evidence presented is convincing and what level of subjectivity or bias exists within the work (Table 2.4). Similarly, Young and Solomon (2009) provide ten questions to ask from a clinical perspective, including whether the study is relevant and adds anything new and if any conflicts of interest exist, which is an important consideration in clinical drug trials (Table 2.5). Other more detailed models provide a greater number of specific questions to be asked within each section of the article (Heller *et al.*, 2008; Seals and Tanaka, 2000).

2.8.1.i Critiquing and changing your professional practice

As noted above there are a large number of critical appraisal tools in the literature. Crowe and Sheppard (2011) compared 44 critical appraisal tools and concluded that users need to be careful about which tool they use and how they use it. The authors later developed their own critical appraisal tool (Crowe *et al.*, 2011a, 2011b). With this in mind an important aspect of critical appraisal is whether you wish to assess the scientific

Table 2.4 Seven questions to ask when critiquing an information source (Deane, 2010)

1. Does the source use primary evidence?
2. Does the source use secondary evidence?
3. Is the evidence convincing?
4. What are the author's credentials?
5. What assumptions does the author make?
6. What subjectivity or bias is evident in the source?
7. Is the language emotive?

Table 2.5 Young and Solomon's ten questions to ask when critically appraising a research article (Young and Solomon, 2009)

1. Is the study question relevant?
2. Does the study add anything new?
3. What type of research question is being asked?
4. Was the study design appropriate for the research question?
5. Did the study methods address the most important potential sources of bias?
6. Was the study performed according to the original protocol?
7. Does the study test a stated hypothesis?
8. Were the statistical analyses performed correctly?
9. Do the data justify the conclusions?
10. Are there any conflicts of interest?

Source: Young, J.M. and Solomons, M.J. (2009) How to critically appraise an article, *Nature Clinical Practice Gastroenterology and Hepatology*, 6, 82–91. Reprinted by permission from Macmillan Publishers Ltd.

rigour of an article (i.e. its quality or internal reliability) or how applicable the work is to your own practices (i.e. its value or external validity) (MacAuley, 1994; Maher *et al.*, 2004). The majority of undergraduate and postgraduate students in Sport and Exercise Science are probably critiquing with respect to scientific rigour as they are generally, but not exclusively, writing an academic piece of work. Conversely, students in areas such as Sports Therapy, and certainly professionals currently in practice, are more likely to be interested in how a piece of research may affect their treatments or clinical practices. The choice of critical appraisal tool is therefore extremely important. The following paragraphs will consider some aspects of both these forms of critical appraisal.

To help assess whether the scientific evidence considered will affect clinical behaviour or the practical approach to treatment, MacAuley (1994) developed the 'READER' aid to critical appraisal. This aid was initially developed for general practitioners with limited time to undertake extensive reviews of the literature (MacAuley, 1994). The 'READER' acronym stands for Relevance, Education, Applicability, Discrimination, Evaluation and Reaction, the main tenets of which are shown in Table 2.6. Each component is given a score and the usefulness of the information is graded according to the total score. This scale has been shown to be valid and reliable and has been used in a range of educational scenarios for general practitioners (Bleakley and MacAuley, 2002; MacAuley, 1996; MacAuley and McCrum, 1999; MacAuley and Sweeney, 1997; MacAuley *et al.*, 1998).

The main reason for introducing this scale here relates to the 'Relevance' component. A key factor of the component stresses that the article is assessed within the reader's own context, highlighting that what is useful for one reader may not be useful for another. Also, your needs may differ over time and in different situations. This is especially true if it has the potential to change your behaviour. Similar tools and appraisal advice have been provided for public health (Heller *et al.*, 2008) and physical therapy (Domholdt *et al.*, 1994; Maher *et al.*, 2004). Students of Sports Therapy may find these useful for the practical aspects of their courses. Even though the focus of these appraisal tools is towards that of potentially altering professional practice they still involve assessing the appropriateness of research questions and hypotheses, study design and the interpretation of results (Heller *et al.*, 2008), as well as the scientific or clinical basis of the work. Don't forget that changing professional practice

Table 2.6 MacAuley's READER aid to the critical appraisal of research articles (MacAuley, 1994)

Component	Main factor(s) and scoring system
Relevance	The article is assessed within the reader's context 1. Not relevant to general practice 2. Allied to general practice 3. Only relevant to specialised general practice 4. Broadly relevant to all general practice 5. Relevant to me
Education	Context of behaviour modification Could it change your behaviour? 1. Would certainly not influence behaviour 2. Could possibly influence behaviour 3. Would cause reconsideration of behaviour 4. Would probably alter behaviour 5. Would definitely change behaviour
Applicability	Can the research be done in the reader's own practice? Can you identify with the practice or circumstances? 1. Impossible in my practice 2. Fundamental changes needed 3. Perhaps possible 4. Could be done with reorganisation 5. I could do that tomorrow
Discrimination	Is the message valid? 1. Poor, descriptive study 2. Moderately good, descriptive study 3. Good descriptive study but methods not reproducible 4. Good descriptive study with sound methodology 5. Single-blind study with attempts to control 6. Controlled single-blind study 7. Double-blind, controlled single-blind study with method problem 8. Double-blind, controlled single-blind study with statistical deficiency 9. Sound scientific paper with minor faults 10. Scientifically excellent paper
Evaluation	If epidemiologically sound, paper should be considered seriously Score based on READ elements
Reaction	Scoring category (NB: the research is not necessarily 'bad', just not for your current needs) 24+ Classic paper which should make an immediate impact on practice 20–23 Paper is of value and filed for immediate access 15–19 Paper may be of interest <15 Paper failed to fulfil the criteria

Source: addpted from MacAuley, D. (1994) READER: an acronym to aid critical reading by general practitioners, *British Journal of General Practice*, 44(379), 83–85, Figure 1.

is not just limited to people working in clinical areas or with patients. The professional practice of sport and exercise scientists includes assessing why you use certain exercise protocols, questionnaires or data collection and analysis techniques. All of these may be affected by what you read in the literature.

2.8.1.ii Critiquing scientific rigour

Most students writing dissertations and compiling literature reviews are probably concerned with the scientific rigour of journal articles. Here, experience in research and writing is invaluable. However, most students will not have developed these skills to a large extent as they are in the early stages of their subject-specific research training. Many of the suggested critique questions within the various published critical appraisal guidelines parallel the advice given for writing literature reviews and the other sections of lab reports, dissertations and research studies. Seals and Tanaka (2000) developed a guide for critiquing scientific articles based upon the forum of postgraduate research seminars. The contents of the guide (Table 2.7) relate to most areas of sport and exercise science whether examined from physiological, psychological or biomechanical perspectives. If we compare this to the general model of critical appraisal the underlying themes are identical, it is the specifics that change with respect to subject discipline.

In conclusion, critical appraisal can take many forms and is specific to the needs of the reader at that time and the task they are set. All of the examples provided and guidelines given are essentially the same but focus on different aspects of critique. For example, Deane's (2010) questions are more general and assess the type of information source reviewed and its validity, whereas Young and Solomon's (2009) questions cover more discipline-specific considerations. Although MacAuley's (1994) critique is focussed mainly on the applicability of research to practice and the potential to change professional behaviour, as with Young and Solomon, the methodological aspects have a large emphasis on the overall score. In this context many reviewers would also have considered the specific points raised by Seals and Tanaka (2000) in evaluating methodological components. Similarly, any scientist assessing the rigour of an experimental design may subsequently decide to use that method. As long as you keep these guidelines and comments in mind, your critical appraisal skills will develop as you read and assess more information sources. Consider the aspects of each model presented here (but note that there are many more available) in relation to the stage of research you are at and put them into practice with the next article you read. Your critique skills and application of knowledge will then quickly develop.

Exercise 2.7

For a journal article obtained from your literature search use the different appraisal methods provided in this chapter to do the following:

1. Determine whether the article is useful for your literature review.
2. Critique the article using the specific criteria of Seals and Tanaka (2000).
3. Determine whether the article will affect what you do with respect to your research design.

Table 2.7 Critiquing a journal article (Seals and Tanaka, 2000)

Section	Questions
Title	Does title accurately reflect the purpose, design, results and conclusions of the study?
Abstract	Succinct, clear, comprehensive summary of the main text of the paper?
	Content consistent with that presented in the main text?
	Data or other key information presented here but not in the main text (or vice versa)?
Introduction	Succinctly states what is known and unknown about the topic?
	Functional, biological and/or clinical significance established?
	Specific experimental question, goal or aim to be addressed stated?
	Previous studies strengths and limitations described?
	Clear how experimental approach will provide unique insight?
Methods	Participants adequately described?
	Population appropriate for the research question?
	Participant number sufficient?
	Population used allow extensive or limited generalisability?
	Assignment of participants to conditions randomised?
	Ethical issues and consent described?
	Design allows hypothesis to be rigorously tested scientifically?
	Proper control groups/conditions included?
	Confounding factors controlled?
	Method described insufficient detail to be repeated?
	Measurement techniques reliable, precise and valid?
	Rationale for measures explained?
	Appropriate data calculation and analysis?
	Statistics appropriate for the study design?
	Statistical assumptions tested/violated?
	Alpha level clearly stated?
Results	Data reported in a clear, concise and well-organised manner?
	Where necessary are standard deviations and standard errors reported (any excess variability)?
	All data presented? Any data presented on any measurement not described in the methods?
	Are all the figures and tables needed?
	Tables and figures properly labelled with correct units and scaled appropriately?
	Any repetition of data in figure and tables?
	Is the data within the expected range?
	How do group differences compare to measurement variability?
Discussion	Major new findings clearly described and properly emphasised?
	Key conclusions adequately supported by the experimental data?
	Is there any alternative way to interpret the data?
	Significance of the results described?
	How do results extend previous knowledge?
	Observations for previous studies described in the context of present results?
	Statements supported by appropriate references?
	Data discussed with insight beyond previously?
	Unique aspects and other experimental strengths properly highlighted?
	Experimental limitations described so as to interpret the results appropriately?
	Suggestions for future work?

Source: Seals, D.R. and Tanaka, H. (2000) Manuscript peer review: a helpful checklist for students and novice referees, *Advances in Physiology Eduction*, June, 23: 52–58.

2.9 Aims, objectives and hypotheses

At the end of the introduction or literature review you will need to state the aim(s) of your experiment. Your aims should follow on smoothly from your literature review and be based on logical reasoning (Thomas and Nelson, 2001). If you have written a clear and informative literature review the reader should have a good idea of what you intend to study or at least where the gaps in the literature exist. Your aim may further be considered to be something that is achievable or a 'resolvable question' (Hopkins *et al.*, 2009). The aim is often expected to be followed by your scientific hypotheses; this is especially true for undergraduate and postgraduate theses. In many cases the aim will be very similar to your title as this reflects what you are investigating. The objectives of a study are often required for final-year projects and essentially relate to what you will do to achieve your aims.

The hypothesis relates to what you think will happen in your study. This should be based upon the information present in your introduction or literature review and therefore previous knowledge. There are two key hypotheses usually presented: the null hypothesis, which states there is no difference between conditions; and the alternate or experimental hypothesis, which states the change in direction or magnitudes of change you expect to find. The null hypothesis is what we are testing statistically. Hence, you may read that researchers have 'rejected their null hypothesis' when a statistically significant result is obtained. A common error is to state that there will be a difference between your conditions but not stating the direction in which you think it may occur. Another common error is stating hypotheses which are not consistent with or that contradict what you have stated in the introduction or literature review.

Many students write their aim and hypotheses of their study quite quickly without much thought for their importance. However, never underestimate how important they are as they underpin everything that you do. Each section of your dissertation has an important link to your aims and hypotheses. For your methods, consider what you are actually testing. Does your study design reflect the question you are actually trying to answer? Do the variables measured reflect the responses in question? For your results, does your analysis examine the appropriate differences or relationships postulated? Within your discussion, are you actually explaining your results with your aims in mind? If not, then you may be off topic. It seems obvious that you would discuss your data in relation to your key research question but this is seldom the case in many first drafts of theses. Table 2.8 gives examples of aims, objectives and hypotheses for the three lab class examples used throughout this text.

Exercise 2.8: Writing aims and hypotheses

Based on the examples given in Table 2.8, write the aims and hypotheses for your lab report or dissertation. Are they consistent with title of your report?

Title: ....

....

Aims: ....

....

Objectives: ....
....
....
....

Null Hypothesis: ....
....
....

Alternative Hypothesis: ....
....
....

Table 2.8 Examples of aims, objectives and hypotheses for the three lab class examples used throughout this book

Lab class	Aim	Objectives	Null hypothesis	Alternative hypothesis
Maximal oxygen uptake	To determine maximal oxygen uptake in running, cycling and arm ergometry.	To measure maximal oxygen uptake during treadmill running, cycling and arm ergometry.	There will be no differences in maximal oxygen uptake between exercise modes.	Maximal oxygen uptake will be greatest during treadmill running and lowest during arm ergometry.
Ground reaction forces	To determine ground reaction forces during walking and running.	To measure ground reaction forces using a force plate. To measure walking and running speed using timing gates.	There will be no differences between ground reaction forces between walking and running.	Ground reaction forces during running will be greater than those during walking.
Anxiety on performance	To determine the effects of anxiety on basketball shooting performance.	To measure basketball shooting performance. To produce high and low anxiety conditions. To measure heart rate in low and high anxiety conditions.	There will be no differences in basketball shooting performance in high and low anxiety conditions.	Basketball shooting performance will be worse in high anxiety conditions.

2.9.1 A note on titles

Having considered the introduction, literature review, aims and hypothesis it would be remiss of us not to consider the actual title of your report! For a lab report this is most likely to be provided in the lab schedule and should describe what has been done within the class – don't just give it the title 'Lab report'. However, for a final-year project your title will probably be determined by you and should reflect your study aims. Most journal guidelines state that a short informative title should be provided, with some authors suggesting that the title should be between 10 and 15 words (Coughlan *et al.*, 2007). However, as Thomas and Nelson (2001) note, a title that is too short may not be very helpful, particularly if it contains 'waste' words such as 'An investigation of' or 'A study of'. Conversely, a title that is too long can become cumbersome and awkward. Consider one of our example lab reports measuring ground reaction forces. A title of 'An examination of ground reaction forces measured from a force plate during walking and running at different speeds on a treadmill in Sports Science students' is too long. A better attempt might be 'Ground reaction forces during treadmill walking and running'. The latter title cuts out extraneous information regarding how the ground reaction forces were measured and who the participants were. However, if the participant population studied was key to the research question then it should be contained in the title, such as '. . . in men and boys'. You should make sure that your key research question is addressed in a clear way.

Your title should not be ambiguous or lead the reader into thinking that you are measuring something different to what you actually are. For example, Seals and Tanaka (2000) give an example of a hypothetical cross sectional study of blood pressure in two groups of people, those with low or high sodium intake. A title such as 'Effects of sodium intake on blood pressure' would be misleading as the study did not involve participants consuming sodium prior to their blood pressure being measured. However, for such a study with a cross sectional design the authors consider 'Blood pressure in humans with low and high sodium intake' to be a much more appropriate title.

2.10 Common problems in writing introductions and literature reviews

If you follow the guidance provided throughout this chapter you will hopefully have fewer errors in your work. However, there are some common mistakes related to the advice above which are worth emphasising. The following points should be read in conjunction with the chapter on 'Referencing and general writing tips' (see Chapter 6).

2.10.1 No clear rationale developed

A lack of focus in your introduction or literature review can be a key problem (Foote, 2006a). Many students do not clearly identify their research question or the rationale for their study and instead provide a general account of facts relating to the overall subject. Indeed, Greenhalgh (1997) notes that, amongst other reasons, journal articles are often rejected by reviewers because the studies do not address an important scientific issue, or because the study was not original, or just because they were badly written. Similarly, Peh and Ng (2010) note the common problems with (invited) literature reviews include a lack of critical evaluation, problems or unresolved areas not being highlighted – which may even be the reason for your own study – and no clear overall message. All of these points are related to developing and clearly communicating the reason for your study. Constructing a clear rationale is therefore not just a problem for undergraduate and postgraduate students.

2.10.2 Writing 'off topic'

This particular error is often linked to no specific rationale being developed and is a common error in the introductions to lab reports. If your writing is going 'off topic' you may still be presenting correct information but it is not relevant to your report area or what was done. In order to counteract this error always have your research question or aims in mind and keep asking yourself 'is this section related to my report?' Students often include statements relating to the methods that are to be undertaken or the tests used. Unless your study is specifically focussing on protocol or procedure development save this information for the methods section. A similar problem exists in writing literature reviews. Here it is most likely that you will initially have various sections that do not help explain your research question or relate to the topic in hand. Don't be worried about deleting large portions of text or sections you have written if they do not relate to your key aims. You can always save it in a different file in case it is useful for another assignment and it will certainly be useful for background knowledge.

2.10.3 Aims, objectives and hypotheses

A key problem with stating the aims of a study or lab report is that they don't relate to what you have presented in the literature review or introduction. If you consider that these statements are setting the scene for your work and providing the scientific reason for the study the aims must be consistent with these. Even when the aims relate to your rationale a common error is that they have no direction. This means that based on what you have stated happens in the introduction or literature review you should have an idea of how your treatment will affect the variables measured. Based on your logical reasoning would you expect a value to increase, decrease or have specific effects?

2.10.4 Under- or over-referencing

Most students know, or are at least taught, that you should always reference the information sources that you use in your work. A common problem, however, and not just in lab reports or projects, is the underuse and overuse of references. With respect to under-referencing, although most lecturers will know which sources the key information you present has come from it is still of paramount importance to acknowledge who has done the work. Stating where your information has come from is of key importance in avoiding plagiarism (for more on this see Chapter 6). You should also remember that your lecturers will know the sources they used within their lectures so don't just cite these, it shows that you haven't looked for other sources yourself. An account with few or no references rings alarm bells that students do not know how to reference or have not used previous literature to develop their research questions or describe their aims.

The opposite of the underuse of references is the overuse of references. This is also a common problem (Foote, 2006a). Although it is essential to reference all your statements and the facts presented, you do not need to cite every study that has investigated or noted your given point. Depending on what you are reporting, choose one or two references which are the most recent, those which are considered influential studies or those which have utilised a similar protocol or technique. As with avoiding using over-wordy or 'flowery' language, don't try to impress by using a large number of references. The person marking your work can see how many sources you have used by looking at your reference list. Just as writing a large number of words is not always better than a shorter concise passage, using a large number of references is not always worth more marks. The appropriateness, interpretation and use of your references are what is important. In addition, consider how the readability is affected by excessive referencing. Too many references in each sentence will certainly affect the flow of your writing.

2.10.5 Overreliance on one or two studies

You may find that one key reference, probably a textbook or review article, will cover all your needs for the range of factors you wish to write about in your introduction. In this case, even though you have referenced appropriately, the same authors will be cited in every sentence, or in a large number of sentences, within a paragraph, which will make you appear over-reliant on just these one or two sources. This is usually more of a problem in the earlier years of your study before you get to grips with using journal articles. However, learning to paraphrase and extract the information you need should reduce this problem. Use original journal articles whenever you can.

2.10.6 Text and subheadings

It is a good idea to use subheadings in your literature review. Subheadings are not required within the introductions of lab reports as this section is limited to a few paragraphs, and in a thesis it is just a few pages. A common error here is when the text does not provide the information that the subheading suggests it should. This can easily be checked when proofreading your work by writing in the margin just one key word that the paragraph covers. If this word does not match the heading, then you should change either the heading or the content.

2.11 Chapter summary and reflections

In this chapter we have considered how to access and extract information to develop a scientific rationale for your introduction or literature review. The focus and content of your introduction or review will depend on the level of study and the requirements of your report. For undergraduate lab reports you will be demonstrating an understanding of key principles and techniques rather than developing a rationale for a novel research study.

Undergraduate and postgraduate dissertations generally have both an introduction and a literature review, whereas lab reports only have an introduction. For final-year projects, you need to consider what the gap in the literature is that has led to your research question, or more simply, what is your area of interest and what hasn't been reported previously? Your rationale should therefore be based upon a critical appraisal of the literature. Once you have identified a gap or gaps in the literature these can be developed into your research question and subsequently your aims and hypotheses. To assess your understanding of introductions and literature reviews answer the following questions:

- What is an introduction?
- How does an introduction differ from a literature review?
- What is critical appraisal or critiquing an article?
- What is a systematic review?
- How do you generate your research question?
- What are the common errors in introductions and literature reviews?

2.12 Further activities

Go to the website of a journal that you regularly read or are aware of. Find the author guidelines and consider the advice given for writing and presenting introductions. See how these differ for review articles in the same journal or for journals specialising in reviews.

Use the critical appraisal tools to evaluate or critique journal articles as you undertake your background reading.

Chapter 3

Methods

In this chapter you will:

- understand the importance of the methods section (Section 3.1)
- appreciate the key components usually reported in the methods (Section 3.2)
- write a section of your methods (Sections 3.3 and 3.7)
- critique part of a section of a methods section (Section 3.8)
- identify common problems when writing methods sections (Section 3.9)

3.1 The importance of a methods section

The methods section (not a methodology, which is a study of methods) is an integral part of your lab report or dissertation and is more important than many students realise. Although the results obtained within the study, the associated conclusions and the take-home message may be of primary importance to the researcher in answering their research question, the process by which they were arrived is just as important (Ng and Peh, 2010b). The methods section should provide full details of how you intend to tackle and answer your research question (Foote, 2008; Kallet, 2004) to enable someone to replicate your study. As such it also provides a medium against which the validity of the study will be judged (Azevedo *et al.*, 2011; Foote, 2008; Huwiler-Müntener *et al.*, 2002; Kallet, 2004). Consider the emphasis placed on the methods section in the critical appraisal section of Chapter 2 (see Section 2.8) and also the recommendation from Kyrgidis and Triaridis (2010) that if the required information is not present within the methods section then journal reviewers should read no further.

This chapter will outline the key components usually expected to be contained within a methods section. If you are writing a lab report you will probably not require all the aspects and details noted here. However, as you progress through your studies to your final-year project, and possibly on to postgraduate studies, all aspects will require your consideration. Depending upon your study and research design some methodological components may require greater description than others. Some components covered here have more relevance to the underlying physiology, biomechanics, psychology or research methods than is simply reported here. If any of these aspects affect your study more than the others you should research them further yourself or consult the literature. As with other chapters in this text, the examples provided will, where possible, reflect the main areas of sport and exercise science and the theme of the three lab reports throughout this text. However, as most undergraduates are likely to have a core of exercise physiology modules to their degree studies the content is (unintentionally) biased towards this area.

3.2 Key components of the methods section

Within the methods section a number of specific aspects should be considered. In general these follow the order of your experiment. For example, you would first determine the research design based on your research question, and gather participant consent and characteristics. You would then, most probably for a dissertation rather than a lab report, undertake some preliminary testing prior to the main experimental trials. Your data would be collected in a predetermined and systematic order and subsequently analysed or processed by known procedures or techniques. Finally, you would analyse your data statistically. Therefore, a typical methods section would normally contain subheadings relating to 'Study design' and 'Participants', which should cover things such as ethics, informed consent and health screening. These sections would then be followed by 'Preliminary trials', including familiarisation, and 'Experimental trials', which is probably the largest subsection and should contain all your data-collection procedures and sample analysis. The final subsection would be 'Statistical analysis'. Exercise 3.1 is designed to start you thinking about potential subheadings for your methods and the order of reporting your methods.

Exercise 3.1: Components of a methods section

Obtain a journal article relating to your project area or, if you are writing up your final-year project, ask your tutor for a previous dissertation. A project that achieved a good grade is best, although one that was not so successful may also help for the purposes of critique. Postgraduate students can generally obtain past dissertations from their supervisor or university library. Read the methods section of your chosen report and consider the order of information. What are the key headings presented?

Key headings:

1. ....

2. ....

3. ....

4. ....

5. ....

Now consider the key areas of your own methods and note down your own potential subheadings.

Potential headings:

1. ....

2. ....

3. ....

4. ....

5. ....

The following subsections do not necessarily reflect the exact subheadings you would use in all lab reports and dissertations but rather reflect a number of important aspects to consider and those which need to be included in the methods wherever possible. Again, it is important to emphasise that not all of these will be required for a lab report where the research design is not necessarily an issue and you may only have one or two participants rather than larger experimental and control groups.

3.2.1 Study design

The design of your research study is the backbone of good research and is much more than simply directing the statistics that are to be used (Knight, 2010). The study design reflects the strategy undertaken to control and manipulate variables to help answer your research question (Kallet, 2004). Subsequently, a great deal of importance should be placed upon the design used (Ng and Peh, 2010b). Azevedo *et al.* (2011) suggest starting with a general paragraph to set the scene for the study design and main characteristics of the study. As was suggested in the introduction and literature review chapter (see Chapter 2), you should keep your research question in mind at all times. Consider all the factors taught in your research methods classes with respect to study design. What kind of study do you have? Do your participants act as their own controls in a repeated measures design, i.e. do they complete a control trial and a treatment trial in a crossover format? Are two separate groups being compared in different conditions? If so, how are they matched? Where possible have you blinded or double blinded your experimental groups? All of these aspects – and potentially many more – are of key importance in assessing the strength of your research design. A summary of common research designs descriptors is shown in Table 3.1 (Hertel, 2010) to help you decide what type of design you have.

Stating the number of trials or conditions undertaken by your participants early on in the methods is helpful for the reader. This provides an insight into the design of your study from the outset. You can then abbreviate your trials to aid the flow of text for the reader. For example, consider the three laboratory classes referred to throughout this book. The following statements could be used in the methods section to provide the reader with initial information regarding the design of those studies.

Lab 1: Maximal oxygen uptake lab

Each participant visited the laboratory on three separate occasions. Each visit involved an incremental exercise test to exhaustion on either the treadmill (TM), cycle ergometer (CE) or arm crank ergometer (ACE).

Lab 2: Ground reaction forces lab

Each participant undertook a range of exercise trials to assess ground reaction forces during walking (WLK) and running (RUN). Due to the short exercise durations and low exercise intensities undertaken all trials were performed on the same day with each trial separated by 10 min of seated rest.

Lab 3: Anxiety and performance lab

Following familiarisation each participant undertook two testing sessions. One involved a low anxiety condition (LOW) and the other a high anxiety condition (HIGH).

Table 3.1 Typical research designs (Hertel, 2010)

Type of study	Description of study design
Meta-analysis	A systematic overview of studies that pools results of two or more studies to obtain an overall answer to a question or interest. Summarises quantitatively the evidence regarding a treatment, procedure or association.
Systematic review	An article that examines published material on a clearly described subject in a systematic way. There must be a description of how the evidence on this topic was tracked down, from what sources, and with what inclusion and exclusion criteria.
Randomised controlled clinical trial	A group of patients is randomised into an experimental group and a control group. These groups are followed up for the variables/outcomes of interest.
Crossover study	The administration of two or more experimental therapies, one after the other in a specified or random order to the same group of patients.
Cohort study	Involves identification of two groups (cohorts) of patients, one that did receive the exposure of interest and one that did not, and follows these cohorts forward for the outcome of interest.
Case-control study	A study that involves identifying patients who have the outcome of interest (cases) and patients without the same outcome (controls) and looks back to see if they had the exposure of interest.
Cross-sectional study	The observation of a defined population at a single point in time or time interval. Exposure and outcome are determined simultaneously.
Case series	Describes characteristics of a group of patients with a particular disease or who have undergone a particular procedure. Design may be prospective or retrospective. No control group is used in the study, although the discussion may compare the results with others published in the literature.
Case report	Similar to the case series, except that only one case or a small group of cases is reported. Descriptive epidemiology study. Observational study describing the injuries occurring in a particular sport.
Controlled laboratory study	An in vitro or in vivo investigation in which one group receiving an experimental treatment is compared with one or more other groups.
Descriptive laboratory study	An in vivo or in vitro study that describes characteristics such as anatomy, physiology or kinesiology of a broad range of subjects or a specific group of interest.
Qualitative study	A study that uses qualitative methods such as grounded theory, phenomenology, ethnography or the case-study approach to understand a phenomenon. Data-collection methods may include participants describing their experiences orally or in writing, or researcher observation of participants' behaviour.

The statements for lab class 1 and lab class 3 inform the reader that each trial was undertaken on a separate visit to the laboratory. For lab class 2 the reader is aware from the start that all trials were performed on the same visit. In these statements it is also useful to note that the participants were familiarised or accustomed to the exercise tests.

3.2.2 Participants or subjects?

Recently there has been a move towards reporting experimental groups as 'participants' rather than 'subjects'. This essentially relates to individuals participating of their own free will rather than being subjected to procedures against their will or without consent. A number of journal articles now state within their author guidelines that participants is their preferred description.

3.2.2.i Participant characteristics

Along with the study design the characteristics of your participants should be one of the first aspects of the method to be covered. For lab reports you may only have data for one person to report instead of a group data set. In case study reports you will most certainly only have specific individuals to consider. Either way, reporting the characteristics of your participant is still important. The standard characteristics usually reported are age, height and body mass. However, you can also report characteristics such as body fat percentage or maximal oxygen uptake ($\dot{V}O_{2max}$) if these are not the main focus of your report. It is also useful, especially for final-year projects, to note the background of the population tested. It is recommended that you describe the participants in the context of the research question (Kallet, 2004). Were they trained or untrained? What training did they do at the time of the study? Has the level of training been consistent for the six or twelve months preceding the study? Were they all from a team sport background or endurance athletes, untrained but otherwise healthy? The benefit of reporting the participant characteristics is that the reader then knows exactly what may be expected of the population in terms of exercise capacity or performance. For example, if you state 'healthy but otherwise untrained' the informed reader will have a good idea as to what the subjects' maximum oxygen uptake mass might be. This is when functional characteristics such as these are useful so the reader can decide for themselves how well trained the athletes were. If your participant characteristics include more than age, height and mass, or if there are more than one group of participants resulting in laborious or confusing sentences for the reader, these data can easily be displayed in a table.

3.2.2.ii Matching groups

Stating the participant characteristics is also important when you have a matched group for comparison. Matching groups means that as many characteristics as possible, except for those distinguishing each specific group, are the same for all participants. For example, you may match groups based on age, body mass, body fat percentage, training backgrounds or characteristics, competitive standard or gender. Closely matching groups reinforces your research question and aids the effectiveness of your experimental groups. It is also important to consider the range of values with each characteristic for the groups tested and whether there is an overlap between groups, especially when fitness or competitive experience are considered.

3.2.2.iii Inclusion and exclusion criteria

Along with the number and selection of participants Ng and Peh (2010b) also consider the population and sampling methods, inclusion and exclusion criteria, and how the control group (if appropriate) was selected. For many undergraduate projects the sample used is often a convenience sample of fellow students or participants from a range of university sports teams. However, inclusion and exclusion criteria should still be set. Inclusion criteria relate to any specific factors that are required to be able to participate in the study. For example, do the participants have to play specific sports, play at a given competitive standard or train a certain number of times per week? In the case of sports therapy projects do participants have to have suffered a certain injury? These factors are important for the application of your results and can increase the validity of your study considerably. Exclusion criteria are not just the opposite of inclusion criteria but relate to factors which mean not all of your potential participants are able to take part. Examples here may be having certain medical conditions. For example, would asthmatics or diabetics be able to take part in your study or would these conditions affect the results in a different way to other participants? Conversely, these conditions may also be used to define the specific population that you are interested in studying.

3.2.3 Ethics, informed consent and health screening

3.2.3.i Ethics

As you read more journal articles you will see that after the participant information has been provided there should be a statement about ethics approval and informed consent. All research studies must have received some form of ethics committee approval to allow data collection to proceed. Reporting ethics considerations is mandatory for published studies (Azevedo et al., 2011) with a number of journals requiring reference to specific statements or guidelines (e.g. Harriss and Atkinson, 2009).

Ethical approval can be obtained through an institutional ethics committee, as in the case of many universities, or through other avenues such as the local health authority or clinically related ethics committees (e.g. the Integrated Research Application System or 'IRAS'; see https://www.myresearchproject.org.uk/). You may have read some published studies noting ethics approval through the 'Institutional Review Board', which is the route taken for ethics application in the United States. You may also see reference to work being 'in accordance with the Helsinki declaration', which ensures that all research is undertaken with, amongst other factors, patient (participant) safety in mind (BMJ, 1996). When considering your ethics application you are also likely to come into contact with the data protection act (http://www.legislation.gov.uk/ukpga/1998/29/contents) and, if using human tissues in any way, the human tissues act (http://www.legislation.gov.uk/uksi/2008/3067/contents/mad). Your tutors can give you further guidance on these important aspects.

Ethical approval is of key importance for undergraduate and postgraduate projects and for all aspects of research undertaken. However, for the laboratory classes you undertake within your taught courses all procedures are likely to be standard or established protocols with an associated risk assessment already undertaken to reduce any potential harm to the participants or experimenter. In this instance you personally will not have had to apply for ethics approval. Consequently, the general procedure for laboratory classes is for participants to complete a health screening questionaire and provide written informed consent.

3.2.3.ii Informed consent, health screening and risk assessment

Once a research study's ethics application has been approved data collection can proceed. Each participant will be given a participant information sheet in which all procedures are clearly outlined using terminology non-experts can understand. Terminology is very important here as not all of your participants will be studying the same degree as you or have the same specific knowledge. Consequently, participants may not understand the tests to be done or the terminology that you use. Once the consent form has been read and the participant is happy to proceed they must sign the informed consent form to state that all aspects of the study have been understood and they understand that they are able to withdraw at any time without question or consequence. This process is usually summarised as 'participants gave written informed consent' and is provided once at the start of the study prior to any experimental testing occurring.

In contrast to informed consent, a health screening form should be completed before every testing session. The health screening form is a declaration of the participant's health at that time and does not usually contain any details regarding the study itself, other than a statement regarding the specific tests or protocols planned for that specific testing session. The health screening form used is likely to be written specifically by your university or research institution based on nationally or internationally recognised guidelines and procedures (e.g. British Association of Sport and Exercise Sciences, American College of Sports Medicine). In your laboratory reports it is important to be specific as to which forms have been completed. The forms used are often confused by undergraduate students and incorrectly reported. A health screening form is completed by every participant prior to any testing session, be it a lab class or project testing session. However, for final-year projects participants complete *one* informed consent form at the start of the study and a health screening form at the start of *every* testing session.

As part of your project ethics application you will most likely have to complete a risk assessment form for the tests and procedures proposed. Here, the term risk refers to all aspects of health and safety and any potential injuries or unexpected events which could occur. As with health screening forms this is usually institution specific and not completed by students for lab classes. This will have been done previously by staff. However, undergraduate students must submit ethics applications for their final-year projects and completing a risk assessment form is an important component. There is always a potential risk when exercising, and it is the measures undertaken to reduce this risk that are important.

3.2.4 Pre-testing considerations

In every methods section you read there will be, or should be, a range of factors considered to try and reduce the amount of variation and error within the data collected. Some general factors are described below but there are likely to be other factors specific to your own study which may potentially contribute to error in your data.

3.2.4.i Circadian rhythms

In research studies that examine performance in some way you will often read that testing occurred at the same time of day but on different days. This is due to the effects of the body's endogenous circadian rhythms on human physiology. Circadian rhythms essentially reflect our body clock with many physiological responses co-varying with changes in body temperature over a 24-hour cycle (Atkinson and Reilly, 1996; Reilly, 2007). There are numerous studies that evaluate the effects of circadian rhythms on performance and you should try and find out whether your protocols and performance measures are affected. This is particularly important if circumstances beyond your control mean that you are unable to test participants at the same time of day on each day. Furthermore, you should always state the amount of rest between testing sessions, for example 'Testing occurred at the same time of day with at least three days between trials'.

3.2.4.ii Diet and physical activity
You will probably be aware of studies into the effect of glycogen depletion on various performance measures (Suriano *et al.*, 2010) as well as affects caused by acute or chronic changes in diet (Maughan *et al.*, 1997; Pitsiladis and Maughan, 1999). As a result of potential changes in performance due to diet and eating behaviour it is important to ensure that your participants maintain both a consistent diet and physical activity pattern during the period of your testing and, importantly, prior to each day of testing. As with reporting the time of day at which testing occurred you will often read a statement to the effect that normal diet was maintained and physical activity was avoided in the 24 hours prior to testing. The latter point may be difficult to enforce when working with athletes, so it may be phrased as 'intense physical activity was avoided'. You can check these potential confounding factors quite simply by using diet and activity questionnaires. However, if you state this has been done you need to note whether the data was specifically analysed or checked visually or verbally.

3.2.4.iii Menstrual Cycle
The majority of physiology textbooks are likely to describe the menstrual cycle with respect to the cyclical changes in sex hormones and body temperature. The range of known physiological responses that occur during the respective phases of the cycle may have subsequent affects on exercise performance. Therefore, the phase of the menstrual cycle of female participants at the time of testing needs to be considered and ideally kept consistent. Such an approach will help ensure that any performance changes are a result of the treatment or intervention rather than varying concentrations of hormones (Burrows, 2007). This is particularly important for your final-year project data collection where testing can be timetabled appropriately, unlike your lab classes. There are a number of recent review articles summarising the physiology of female athletes (Burrows and Bird, 2000; Charkoudian and Joyner, 2004), the effect of the menstrual cycle on various performance measures (Constantini *et al.*, 2005; Janse de Jonge, 2003; Lebrun, 1994) and testing considerations for female athletes (Burrows, 2007). As with circadian rhythms, these should be consulted with respect to your own laboratory tests.

3.2.4.iv Familiarisation to testing procedures
When you are about to begin your data collection it is important to realise that the majority of your participants are unlikely to have experienced the exact test procedures before, unless they are on your degree course and have experienced the same lab classes or have been involved in previous research studies. Therefore, it is essential to familiarise, or accustom (Winter, 2005), your participants to the protocols and techniques required. Consider exercising for the first time wearing a face mask or using a mouthpiece and nose clip for the analysis of expired gas or undertaking a test

of maximal exertion. How would this feel, especially for less-fit participants? For psychological or motor skill studies involving tests of reaction time or some form of cognitive function test it is likely that participants will improve their performance over the first few attempts. If participants are not given time to practice the tests and an improvement in performance is observed in your results, this could simply be due to a learning effect rather than a true experimental affect. Many authors will therefore state that 'participants were fully familiarised with all procedures prior to testing'. It is important here to give as much detail as you can with respect to how this was done.

Although it is considered good lab practice to ensure that participants are accustomed to all procedures, the specific effects of this process are not widely reported. However, the effects of familiarisation have been considered for a range of performance tests including canoeing and cycling time trials (Corbett et al., 2009; Sealey et al., 2010), repeated sprints (McGawley and Bishop, 2006; Spencer et al., 2006) and prolonged exercise containing performance components (Marino et al., 2002; Tyler and Sunderland, 2009). Improvements in performance following one (Sewell and MaGregor, 2008), three (Marino et al., 2002; Tyler and Sunderland, 2009) or four trials (Sealey et al., 2010) have been noted along with alterations in pacing strategy (Corbett et al., 2009; Tyler and Sunderland, 2009). Therefore, failure to provide your participants with an opportunity to become accustomed to your study procedures could have a significant effect on your results.

Exercise 3.2: Your methodological considerations

For each of the factors listed below consider how you have overcome any potential limitations or how you have controlled for them. Not all of these factors will be of importance to your study, especially for lab reports, but it is worth considering how many are and how they could affect your data or comparisons.

	How important?	Key information required
Participant characteristics	....	....
Circadian rhythms	....	....
Diet and physical activity	....	....
Menstrual cycle	....	....
Familiarisation	....	....

3.3 General reporting of procedures

As noted earlier the methods section should provide all the information required to allow a researcher to repeat the experiment. Although the methods section can be likened to a recipe (Foote, 2008) it is not a step-by-step tutorial (such as in a lab schedule) but a systematic and complete description of the work done (Azevedo et al., 2011). A common error is to include extraneous information that does not aid the description of your procedures. Kyrgidis and Triaridis (2010) suggest that there are four levels of reporting methods: (1) those known to everyone; (2) those which are less common but well documented; (3) those which are relatively uncommon; and (4) those which are developed by the researchers and should be described in detail

Four levels of reporting methods:

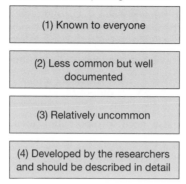

Figure 3.1 Four levels of reporting methods
Source: Kyrgidis and Triaridis (2010)

(Figure 3.1). If a novel method is being introduced this will require a full description and discussion (Kallet, 2004). Indeed, the whole purpose of your study may be developing a new exercise protocol, questionnaire or method and assessing its validity and reliability. In this instance a clear description of what was done is of paramount importance. For most undergraduate lab reports the methods used are likely to be well established and you should consider reporting all the important elements to illustrate your knowledge of the techniques used. Details should be provided of all exercise protocols undertaken, measurements made and at what time points they were recorded. For dissertations a schematic diagram (see Section 3.6) is often useful for this, especially where a large number of measures are taken and a large number of time points are involved, with the written description being potentially lengthy.

An important consideration of the methods section is where procedures are based on any assumptions or rationales. This is particularly true when variables can only be approached indirectly (Kallet, 2004). A good example of this is indirect calorimetry to determine oxygen uptake and/or energy expenditure values. Most descriptions of these procedures will consider what is actually measured by the researcher rather than any underlying assumptions. Students are assumed to have a level of knowledge commensurate with their level of study. For example, it is important to show an understanding of cardiorespiratory variables in first-year degree studies by defining stroke volume and cardiac output or how to calculate respiratory exchange ratio. However, in your final year of study, providing information such as this is generally not required as it is expected knowledge. Instead, you would probably be expected to comment on more complex adaptations to variables such as end diastolic volume, pre-load, left ventricular diameter, etc. Always check with your tutor if you are unsure. A good rule of thumb is to use any definitions provided in your lectures. If definitions are not given there, you should assume that you are expected to know it!

3.3.1 Describing exercise protocols

Within the sport and exercise sciences most projects will involve some form of exercise or movement. This section is therefore biased towards some of the most commonly used exercise protocols you will encounter. Nevertheless, the principles are the same whether you are reporting physiology, biomechanics or psychology-based studies.

3.3.1.i Typical exercise protocols

When reporting your exercise protocols it is important to appreciate the different terminology used to describe them. For example, the typical test for maximal oxygen uptake ($\dot{V}O_{2max}$) is incremental exercise (meaning increasing in intensity) to volitional exhaustion. The protocol may be continuous or discontinuous and is usually straightforward to describe. You need to consider the initial power output or treadmill velocity, the magnitude of increases in power output or velocity with each stage, the duration of each stage and any rest periods undertaken between stages. For cycling and arm cranking studies you also need to report the cadence or crank rate used (i.e. rev.min^{-1}). If you are using a protocol from a previous study you can reference this, but it is still useful to provide a description of what was undertaken or key factors in the protocol design. For example:

> Participants undertook an incremental test to volitional exhaustion to determine maximal oxygen uptake (Price and Halabi, 2005). This protocol involved an initial velocity of 8 km.h^{-1} for 5 minutes followed by increment of one km.h^{-1} every minute

or

> Maximal oxygen uptake was determined from an incremental treadmill test (Price and Halabi, 2005).

Other aspects of protocols can also be referenced. A common aspect of treadmill protocols is to set the gradient at 1% in order to elicit the same energy cost as running outdoors (Jones and Doust, 1996).

When considering multiple sprints or intermittent exercise definitions can get a little more confusing. For example, 'multiple sprints' usually refers to short duration, maximal sprints similar to that of the Wingate Anaerobic Test (participants sprinting as fast as possible for 30 seconds against a resistive load of 7.5% body mass) but of shorter duration and with a set recovery between sprints. The model of 10×6 seconds repeated sprints has commonly been used to examine multiple sprint responses during cycling (Gaitanos et al., 1991), running (Hamilton et al., 1991) and arm cranking (Artioli et al., 2007).

A number of exercise protocols use the term 'intermittent exercise'. This term refers to exercise with rest periods in between exercise bouts or a range of exercise intensities simulating team sports. The exercise could be of high intensity such as that undertaken by athletes during interval training (Helgerud et al., 2007; Rozenek et al., 2007; Seiler and Hetlelid, 2005), of low intensity such as used in more clinical scenarios (Bougault et al., 2005; Campbell et al., 2011) or a mixture of intensities to simulate team sport activities (Drust et al., 2000; Nicholas et al., 2000). It is useful here to describe the specific exercise undertaken together with an indication of the exercise intensity. For example, a large number of studies have examined responses to 'high-intensity shuttle running' (Morris et al., 2000; Sunderland and Nevill, 2003, 2005). Specific exercise definitions favoured by your tutors will no doubt be provided in lectures or laboratory manuals so it is always best to follow those.

3.3.1.ii Ergometers

A range of ergometers are available for exercise testing. The word 'ergometer' comes from 'ergo' meaning 'work' and 'meter' meaning 'to measure'. In my years of marking laboratory reports I have come across a range of descriptions and spellings, for example, ergo meter, ergonometer and cycling machine. The most common mistake relates to the term cycle ergometer. The standard cycle ergometer has one wheel and should not be called a bicycle ergometer. Bicycles have two wheels. A confounding factor to describing ergometers, and one that probably adds to the confusion, is that the word 'ergometer' is not generally recognised by spell checkers, so it is likely to be highlighted in your word-processing document as incorrect. This doesn't mean that it is spelled incorrectly, however, just that is it not in standard use.

3.3.1.iii Describing techniques and procedures

Expired gas analysis Using the correct descriptors for your various processes is important to demonstrate understanding of the technique. For example, one of the most common techniques used in undergraduate sport and exercise science is that of collecting and analysing expired gas. First, note that the samples collected are termed expired gas rather than expired air. This may seem pedantic, but air is a known concentration of components (20.9% oxygen and 79.0% nitrogen, together with small quantities of carbon dioxide and inert gasses) whereas the gas breathed out is of unknown concentrations, although admittedly within a known or expected range, hence it is measured and not assumed.

Many published studies have well-described sections regarding the collection and analysis of expired gas samples using the Douglas bag technique. It is not the purpose of this chapter to overview the procedure but rather to ensure that what is written within your methods section makes sense to the reader. Key errors of description are usually centred around the process itself, which involves collecting samples, analysing them and calculating the desired values (i.e. minute ventilation, oxygen consumption, carbon dioxide production and respiratory exchange ratio). The gas samples are analysed using gas analysers which provide measures of the fraction of expired gas that is oxygen (F_EO_2) or carbon dioxide (F_ECO_2). The analysers themselves do not directly provide measures of oxygen consumption and carbon dioxide production. Values for these latter variables are obtained from subsequent calculations often using in-house software. Therefore, descriptions will often state that 'expired gas was analysed for fractions of oxygen and carbon dioxide with oxygen consumption, carbon dioxide and respiratory exchange ratio being subsequently calculated'.

Another common mistake is stating that 'gas volume and temperature were measured using a dry gas meter'. Dry gas meters do not measure temperature, they measure gas volume. Gas temperature is measured using a thermistor or other device within the system. Using the correct wording for a given process will certainly improve the clarity of your descriptions.

Force plate and motion analysis Biomechanics reports often require some quite technical descriptions. When force plates or cameras for motion analysis are used it is important to note the number and type of cameras, and how the data was collected and processed. Reporting how data was treated is also important for data such as electromyography (EMG) recordings, particularly when a range of methods may be available and used by different authors. For example, if collecting force plate data consider the following:

Ground reaction forces were measured by means of a force plate (Kistler Force Plate 9281B, Kistler Instruments, Switzerland). The three force components (X, Y and Z) were amplified and converted from analogue to digital signals. Data was recorded on a personal computer at a sampling frequency of 1000 Hz. The changes in the resultant force vector as measured by the centre of pressure (COP) and corresponding area, path, velocity, frequency and amplitudes were calculated. Data acquisition and processing was undertaken using Vicon Workstation® (Vicon Peak Workstation®, Oxford Metrics, UK) (Hill *et al.*, unpublished data).

If collecting motion camera data consider the following:

Six Vicon infrared motion capture video cameras were positioned around the participants. Cameras were set on tripods and operated at a frequency of 50 Hz. Prior to testing the system was calibrated in order to allow the software to calculate the relative location and orientation of the cameras and to define the three-dimensional coordinate system. Eight light reflective caption markers (Vicon, Oxford Metrics, UK) were placed on selected bony landmarks on the right-hand side of the body (greater tuberosity, olecranon process, ulnar styloid, spinous tubercles, anterior superior iliac spine, mid femur, lateral condyle and lateral malleolus) for analysis of the kinematic responses. The distance between each marker and the markers position relative to the bony landmark was measured and recorded for subsequent trials. All reflective markers captured were subsequently identified and labelled. Data were exported into an Excel file for further analysis of joint movements (Hill *et al.*, unpublished data).

Metabolites   Various methods for the analysis of metabolites may also be referenced by the author as the full procedures can be quite lengthy. Blood glucose and lactate concentrations, if not analysed using hand-held portable monitors or bench-based instruments, can be analysed spectrophotometrically using commercially available assays or standard procedures, respectively. However, if you were writing an analytical style paper based around an analysis method then specific biochemical assays or formulae are of greater importance. If writing a thesis such specific aspects should be added to the appendices.

3.3.1.iv Questionaires and scales

Where questionnaires are involved it is imperative to state who it was developed by, the version used and any comments regarding its validation. For example, there are a large number of scales for assessing anxiety or personality. It is not sufficient to just state 'personality was assessed using a questionaire' or 'anxiety was assessed by standard procedures'.

As well as questionaires there are also a range of perceptual scales used within sport and exercise science. Here, verbal descriptors are attached to a number on a finite scale. The best-known scale of this type is for ratings of perceived exertion (RPE), which is measured by the Borg Scale (Borg, 1973). When considering RPE there are different scales for different types of RPE (overall or differentiated) or versions developed for specific clinical populations (Noble and Robertson, 1996). Other scales include 'Readiness to Exercise' (Nurmekivi *et al.*, 2001) and 'Ratings of Perceived Thermal Strain' (Young *et al.*, 1987). As with questionnaires it is important to note who developed the scale that has been used and whether it has been validated.

3.3.1.v Stating formulae

As with exercise protocols there is a range of techniques used which have standard components. For example, when assessing body composition using the skinfold method, it is frequently cited that body fat was calculated using the formula of Durnin and Womersley (1974) or through densitometry techniques using the formulae of Siri (1961) or Brozek *et al.* (1963). Although the actual formulae and procedures are well known it is good practice to include them. Where formulae are relatively straightforward, such as in studies of thermoregulation calculating mean skin temperature (Ramanathan, 1964), the formula can easily be stated in the method. Where a less common or less well-known procedure is undertaken the formula should always be provided. For example, during studies examining the effectiveness of hand cooling on performance the amount of heat lost from the hands to water during the hand-cooling procedure is calculated using the method of Livingstone *et al.* (1989). As this formula is less well known it should be provided and the components listed or defined.

3.3.1.vi Presumed procedures

It is important to note that many statements regarding equipment preparation are often presumed or expected to have occurred. Many students include discursive or superfluous statements to try and demonstrate that they have a good appreciation of what has been done. Common statements include: 'Douglas bags were evacuated before use' – although this is clearly important before collecting samples it is standard procedure and is expected to have occurred; 'Data was recorded in a results sheet' – again, where data has been noted it is expected to have been written down or recorded somewhere; and 'Equipment was checked before use to ensure it was working properly'. This would be inherent in the calibration procedures, many of which will probably be done before each laboratory class without the students being aware of them. If the laboratory class is, for example, based around calibration procedures or producing a dose–response curve to determine the solute content of given samples, such procedures are important to describe.

3.3.1.vii Naming equipment

Within your methods section it is imperative that sufficient information is given so that the study could be repeated. It is common practice to name the piece of equipment used for each variable (or groups of variables) measured. As different analysers and equipment exist to measure your variables there is potential for different calibration methods, etc. to be undertaken. The reader will then know specifically what equipment was used to collect and analyse the data and they can then form their own opinion as to its appropriateness, reliability and validity. More specifically it is standard to provide the name of the equipment, the city and country of origin. For example, 'Exercise was performed on a cycle ergometer (Monark 814E, Varberg, Sweden)' or 'Heart rate was continuously monitored using a heart rate monitor (Polar Electro, Kempell, Finland)'.

3.3.2 Nomenclature and units

The majority of journals will often refer authors to an excepted list of standard units or 'SI units'. The 'SI' refers to the '*Système International*' or in its full form '*Le Système*

International d'Unités' and is the modern metric system of measurement (Thompson and Taylor, 2008). As with most standard references these are available in pdf format from various websites (e.g. The International Bureau of Weights and Measures). Examples of the use of SI units are seconds (s) for time, metres (m) for length and kilogrammes (kg) for mass. There are also a number of non-SI units which are often used and are accepted for use within the International System of Units, e.g. minute (min), hour (h) and litre (l) (Thompson and Taylor, 2008).

Some variables do not have units or may be expressed as ratios or 'arbitrary units'. Ratios represent one variable in proportion to another. A good example is work to rest ratios, such as 60 seconds of exercise followed by 30 seconds of rest. Here the work to rest ratio is 60:30 or 2 (i.e. 60/30). Here the units have to be the same and are effectively cancelled out in the calculation. The other main ratio variables within sport and exercise science are pH and respiratory exchange ratio (RER). Similarly, with respect to units, the Borg Scale for ratings of perceived exertion (Borg, 1973) does not have units. It is worth noting that the Borg scale provides a 'rating' and not a 'rate' and it reports 'exertion' not 'exhaustion'. In some studies you may see data reported in Arbitrary Units or International Units (IU), which represents analysis based on relative changes.

3.3.2.i Formatting

With the use of word processing being widespread throughout universities and colleges for the production of laboratory reports and dissertations there is no reason why more complex formatting applications available within word processing packages can't be used. Many word processers have equation options that facilitate the production of professional-looking (and correct) equations and formulae. Admittedly, being required to produce complex chemical formulae or mathematical equations is relatively uncommon in sport and exercise science; however, there are a number of formatting options which will be of tremendous use. The key ones are subscripts and superscripts and the use of $\dot{V}$ rather than V.

3.3.2.ii Subscripts and superscripts

Subscripts are smaller characters typeset at a lower level than the main characters, for example $\dot{V}O_2$ or $\dot{V}O_{2max}$. These can simply be achieved by typing '$\dot{V}O2$' as normal in the document, highlighting the required text and applying the subscript option, usually from the formatting menu. The same can be done for superscripts, which are smaller characters at a higher level than the main characters. These are most common in addressing variable units such as $beats.min^{-1}$ or $litres.min^{-1}$. Many students do use subscripts and superscripts but not always in the right way. For example, which is correct: O_2 or O^2? A common mistake is to type the number 2 as a superscript rather than a subscript – usually this can be remedied during proofreading. The different positions though do mean very different things in terms of the molecules chemical properties so it is important to get them right.

When letters have a dot above them it infers that there is a time element to the unit of measurement; in other words it is a rate. For example, $\dot{V}$ is often used in conjunction with minute ventilation, oxygen consumption or carbon dioxide production giving $\dot{V}E$, $\dot{V}O_2$ and $\dot{V}CO_2$, respectively. These variables have units of litres per minute and therefore have both a volume and a time base in their measurement. Similarly, cardiac output is also measured in litres per minutes so is generally represented by $\dot{Q}$. The procedures for producing these symbols are straightforward and given in the appendices (see Appendix 2).

3.4 Validity, reliability and biological variation

3.4.1 Validity and reliability

All the procedures that you use should be valid. This means that they should measure what they purport to measure. Procedures should also be reliable or repeatable. In other words, when you repeat the test or measure after an appropriate duration of time and under the same conditions you should expect to get the same results. If conditions under which your tests are undertaken are the same for both tests (sometimes referred to as 'test re-test') this gives a measure of your own variability in undertaking the test and therefore how reliable the test is when you undertake it, i.e. what your level of error is. Consider the example of a group of familiarised participants undertaking a Wingate anaerobic test on two separate occasions with a week separating each test (producing peak power values of 829 ± 54 Watts and 845 ± 48 Watts for test one and test two, respectively). If you calculated the difference between tests for each participant and the subsequent mean difference for the group (e.g. 16 ± 26 Watts) you would then have calculated the bias or expected variation between tests. This procedure is actually part of the calculation for the Limits of Agreement in assessing the repeatability of measures (Bland and Altman, 1986, 1995). You can then use this value to help analyse the variation in your data and the meaningfulness of your data. In other words, differences between tests or treatments of greater than 16 W may be biologically important. However, for lab reports establishing the error is unlikely to be a key focus of the class as you are learning to use equipment and processes (which may go wrong) which are just as important as the data collected. Likewise, for your final-year project data although you would be expected to have practiced the required techniques you would not have the time for an in-depth assessment of measurement error. However, postgraduate students would be expected to report the reliability or typical error of their measurements. Clearly, the lower the error the more accurate the data and the greater the potential for observing significant differences.

As well as informing you about the accuracy of your data collection and reporting the reproducibility (reliability) of your techniques, assessing the variability is important in discussing how meaningful any change in your variables actually is. There is a wide range of factors contributing to the error of your data collection. Usually, the more steps there are in the analysis procedures the greater the potential for error to exist. However, once you are well practiced at a technique your measurement error should be considerably reduced and certainly more consistent. Although manufacturers will usually provide data for the reproducibility of their operating procedures you should always determine your own values. The repeatability of data is not only important for physiological or biochemical variables. Questionaires need to be properly developed and psychometrically tested on or for the population you are testing (Kyrgidis and Triaridis, 2010). Using the appropriate scales for your participants is an extremely important component of the validity of the data collected (Brink and Louw, 2011).

3.4.2 Biological variation

From the factors described above you can see that there are a number of components contributing to your measurement error or measurement variability. However, there is also biological variability. To put this into context, if you were to measure your resting heart rate every morning, would it always be exactly the same? For psychological variables, is your mood the same every day? Would your muscle activity and recruitment of fibres be exactly the same for a given movement? Would your technique for a given skill always be exactly the same? The answer here is no and the differences are predominantly due to biological variability. In determining the biological variation in $\dot{V}O_{2max}$ assessments Katch *et al.* (1982) reported that both biological variation and technological error amounted to ±5.6%. However, 90% of this variation was biological variation. Similarly, when assessing biological variation in residual lung volume measurement and the subsequent effect on body fat percentage values, Marks and Katch (1986) calculated that biological variance accounted for 72% of within-subject variance.

Controlling for circadian rhythms, menstrual cycle and learning effects can all help to reduce the biological variation. However, other factors can also affect a participant's performance. For example, improvements in performance of a range of exercise tests have been observed when verbal encouragement has been provided (e.g. Wingate performance, Karaba-Jakovljević *et al.*, 2007; elbow flexor strength, McNair *et al.* 1996) and when the encouragement is more frequent (maximal treadmill test, Andreacci *et al.*, 2002). Therefore, when undertaking performance tests strong verbal encouragement is often provided and stated in the method. This process should also be standardised as far as possible. Wherever possible you should state how random errors and systematic errors were reduced (Kyrgidis and Triaridis, 2010).

3.5 Calibration

Having briefly considered validity and reliability and the factors that contribute to them we will now consider equipment calibration. Calibration of your equipment is extremely important as it ensures that the readings from your equipment or analysers are accurate. For example, common procedures requiring calibration prior to analysis include blood variables such as blood lactate and blood glucose concentrations and gas analysers for the determination of oxygen and carbon dioxide concentrations. Calibration essentially involves the output from the analyser being comparing to a known value or standard. If the difference between values is within acceptable limits then the calibration is usually accepted and the results obtained should be accurate. Many calibration procedures use a two-point calibration (i.e. two known values) as the electrical output from many analysers in response to different samples is linear. However, the more values you check the more confident you can be that your data is accurate. Analysing a standard solution as your first proper sample is a good way to check this. Use of a range of known values or standards can provide you with what is termed a 'linearity check'. In addition, the standards used usually reflect the physiological range of values expected (e.g. for expired gas, 15% oxygen and 5% carbon dioxide; for blood lactate between 1 and 10 mmol.l^{-1}).

Calibration checks can provide you with information regarding the normal variation of your measurements. If you were to get a difference between mean blood lactate concentrations of 0.5 mmol.l^{-1} and your own error compared to a known sample is 0.2 mmol.l^{-1} then the difference is greater than your error and this could be due to your experimental treatment. For undergraduate lab reports you will not personally have to calibrate equipment (with the exception of some exercise protocols such as the Wingate anaerobic test) as it will already have been done by technical staff. However, postgraduate students are responsible for the calibration of their own equipment. When reporting calibration procedures many authors state the reference standards used and that all procedures were calibrated in accordance with the manufacturer's guidelines.

3.6 Use of schematics

For many undergraduate and postgraduate dissertations as well as some journal articles the experimental procedures can be helpfully represented using some form of schematic diagram, particularly when there are a large number of variables or time points considered or where the design is more complicated. Diagrams are unlikely to be required for laboratory classes or where your project has a relatively straight-forward design (experiments don't have to be complicated to be informative and worthwhile!). Schematics are usually a must for any oral presentation of your work and are very helpful in explaining procedures to an audience. Schematic diagrams are also useful in helping you plan out your protocol and are extremely useful to have to hand during your first few experimental trials. The latter ensures that you don't miss any data collection points when testing. An example of a schematic for an intermittent exercise protocol is given in Figure 3.2.

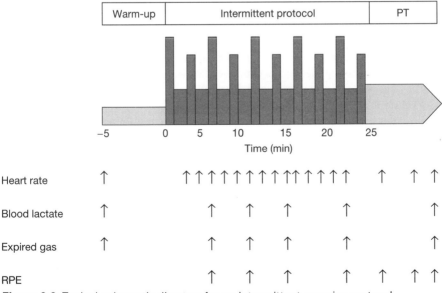

Figure 3.2 Typical schematic diagram for an intermittent exercise protocol.
PT = performance trial.

Exercise 3.3: Developing a schematic of your experimental protocol

If your experimental protocol is quite involved this exercise may help you finalise your measurement times or explain your method. To help you develop a schematic of your protocol list the variables that you are going to measure and the corresponding measurement time points. An example for both heart rate and blood lactate concentration are provided.

Variable	Measurement time point
Heart rate	Rest, post warm-up, every 5 min of exercise, at exhaustion
Blood lactate concentration	Rest, 5, 15, 30 minutes of exercise, after performance trial
....	....
....	....
....	....
....	....
....	....
....	....
....	....
....	....
....	....

3.7 Statistical analysis

The statistical analysis section should be the last section of your methods section (Knight, 2010). You should ensure that the analysis is consistent with the first section of the methods relating to study design and your research question. Within this section it is important to state any data manipulation (e.g. combining data, calculation of delta or 'change' variables), the statistical tests used, and both the statistical package and specific procedures used within the package (Knight, 2010). There is usually an initial statement noting that data is expressed as means and standard deviations along with any checks of data normality and distribution. You should then list the statistical tests (often in the order of complexity) and any differences to standard techniques applied. You are likely to have used the same statistical test for a number of variables so these can easily be grouped together. Try Exercise 3.4 and read the examples provided. (If you are not confident with statistics you may find it helpful to read the next chapter covering the results section of reports and also consult your supervisor.)

Exercise 3.4: Describing your statistical analysis

With respect to the points noted in Section 3.7 write down the key tests that you are likely to use or have used in the analysis of your data. It may be helpful to consider this in relation to your research question or specific hypotheses and each variable measured. You can then organise or group your statistical tests ready for your description in the methods section.

Variable measured	Statistical analysis
....	....
....	....
....	....
....	....
....	....
....	....
....	....
....	....
....	....
....	....

Example statistical descriptions for each of the lab reports used throughout this book could include the following:

Lab 1 Maximal oxygen uptake

Data are expressed as means and standard deviations. Maximal oxygen uptake and maximal heart rate were analysed using one way analysis of variance (ANOVA). Significance was accepted at the level of $P < 0.05$. Where significance was obtained Tukey post-hoc analysis was undertaken. All data were analysed using the statistics function in Microsoft Excel.

Lab 2 Ground reaction forces

All data are expressed as mean ± standard deviation. The walking and running speeds achieved in each trial and the corresponding peak ground reaction forces were analysed using one way analysis of variance (ANOVA) using Microsoft Excel. Significance was accepted at the level of $P < 0.05$. Where significance was obtained Tukey post-hoc analysis was undertaken as outlined by Vincent (1999). Correlations between body mass and ground reaction force were analysed using Pearson's correlation coefficient.

Lab 3 Anxiety and performance

All data are expressed as mean ± SD. Basketball shooting performance and mean heart rate during each trial were analysed using two way analysis of variance (ANOVA) with repeated measures on both factors (anxiety × experience). Significance was accepted at the level of $P < 0.05$. Where significance was obtained Tukey post-hoc analysis was undertaken. All data were analysed using PASW (version 17, Chicago).

3.8 'General methods' sections

Although all PhDs are different with respect to the scientific approach and the number of experimental studies undertaken all will have a number of studies which are linked together to help answer the main research question. As such there are often many common procedures or protocols undertaken across each study. To prevent repetition in the thesis it is quite acceptable to present a general methods chapter which considers all these procedures together in one section. However, if you find that only factors such as ethics and participant recruitment or preliminary testing procedures are common you may find it best to describe these in each section or potentially refer to the first study where they are reported (check with your supervisory team for preference). A general methods section is also the ideal place in which to present your calibration procedures, validation and reliability data and general procedures such as participant familiarisation. Presenting these aspects also helps to demonstrate a good understanding and awareness of the research process, data collection and generally good science. When you are writing up your thesis you may find this is a useful section to consider.

3.9 Writing your methods and common errors

As noted in Section 3.3 the methods section is often compared to a recipe (Foote, 2008), providing sufficient detail to repeat the experiment (Ng and Peh, 2010b). In addition, the order of the methods section should be written in a systematic way, usually in the order that the study was carried out (Ng and Peh, 2010b). For final-year undergraduate students, postgraduate students and the majority of researchers the methods section is likely to have already been written to some extent prior to data collection as it will have been included in research proposals and ethics application (Azevedo *et al.*, 2011). There may be minor changes to add once pilot testing has been completed (ethics permitting) but the key procedures are likely to be written. However, to aid the development and reporting of your method the exercises in this chapter have considered key sections or potential subheadings within the method, a range of preliminary testing considerations, planning and description using schematics, and describing your statistical analyses. In addition, there are a number of factors for less-experienced researchers to consider when writing undergraduate laboratory reports, and a range of these are considered below.

3.9.1 Length of the methods section

A common question from students is 'How long should my methods section be?' The simple answer is as long as it takes to describe all the procedures undertaken in relation to the marking criteria. Concern often arises when students talk to each other regarding their project write-ups but fail to realise that the methods for some projects are more straightforward in their design and description than others so will have a shorter methods section. Always consult your supervisor for specific feedback.

3.9.2 Past tense, third person

Methods sections are written in what is referred to 'past tense, third person'. With respect to past tense, the way to appreciate this is that when reading your completed lab report or project the study has already been done, and is therefore in the past. For example, you should state 'On arrival at the laboratory height and body mass *were* recorded' or 'Personality *was* assessed using . . .' not 'On arrival to the laboratory height and body mass *will* be recorded' or 'Personality *will* be assessed using . . .'. The latter examples are future tense. Your research proposal will have been written in future tense as the study had not yet happened. However, a good proofread should overcome any lapses in wording if you have cut and pasted information from your proposal to your method. As regards third person, this takes out the 'personal touch'. A common student mistake is to state that '*We* measured body mass' rather than stating that 'Body mass was measured'. Once you get used to reporting the procedures in this way it is quite easy to reproduce in subsequent reports.

3.9.3 Only include methods information

As with other sections of lab reports and projects a common error is to include information that does not aid the description of your procedures or the inclusion of your results (Foote, 2008). Essentially, what is learned within the study should be contained in the results not the methods. Furthermore, if you have a large amount of information to justify particular methods, it may be more appropriate to include a section in your introduction or literature review covering this.

3.9.4 Terminology

Appropriate terminology has been covered in the 'General reporting of procedures' section (see Section 3.3). An important point to re-emphasise here is the need to describe the equipment used, such as not referring to analysers or instruments as machines.

Exercise 3.5: Critique part of a methods section

Using a journal article from your literature searches read the methods section and determine whether the study is clearly explained and whether it could easily be replicated. Also, consult the section on critical appraisal earlier in the text (see Chapter 2, Section 2.8) to critique the methods section. What can you take from this appraisal to help improve your own writing?

Key factors to consider and improve

1. ....

2. ....

3. ....

4. ....

5. ....

6. ....

7. ....

8. ....

9. ....

10. ....

3.10 Chapter summary and reflection

This chapter covered a range of factors that you should consider reporting within your methods section and should also be aware of with respect to your research design. The typical procedures and forms required before a study can be undertaken were also noted. Although you may have already collected your data prior to reading this chapter the factors described may be useful in explaining the responses you obtained in relation to variability of your data. For lab reports where testing sessions will have timetable and participant constraints these factors are likely to be less of an issue but are still important for understanding your data. This chapter also considered how to plan and write your method with respect to common errors in student reports. To assess your understanding of methods sections answer the following summary questions:

- What is the purpose of a methods section?
- What aspects are routinely reported in methods sections?
- How do your methods reflect your research question or hypothesis?
- What are the common errors when writing methods sections?

3.11 Further activities

Go to the website of a journal that you regularly read or are aware of. Find the author guidelines and consider the advice given for writing methods sections.

Use the critical appraisal tools in the chapter on introductions (see Chapter 2) to evaluate or critique journal articles as you undertake your background reading. Also, use these points to critique your own work.

Consult your lab schedule and ensure that you understand each procedure you are undertaking. It will also be helpful to determine the reliability, the expected values and daily variation of each protocol you use from previous literature.

Chapter 4

Results

In this chapter you will be able to:

- appreciate the purpose of the results section   (Section 4.1)
- present data graphically   (Section 4.2)
- present data in tables   (Section 4.3)
- choose appropriate statistical tests to analyse your data   (Section 4.4)
- write and critique a results section   (Section 4.4)
- identify common errors in results sections   (Section 4.6)

4.1 Purpose of the results section

The chief purpose of the results section is to present the data you have collected in a clear, concise and meaningful way. Your results section will usually include some combination of figures or tables, the outcomes of any statistical analysis and a written description of the main findings. There are a number of ways in which you could present your data once it has been analysed. Each method has its own advantages and disadvantages, but however you present your results they should be organised in a logical order (Foote, 2009b; ICMJE, 1997). This chapter is designed to give guidance as to the best ways of presenting your data, how to be consistent in your approach and to highlight common errors in data presentation.

4.2 Presenting data graphically

Different authors have different opinions about what is the best way to present data. However, some figures lend themselves to certain types of data more effectively than others. The main types of figures presented in laboratory reports include block graphs, line graphs and various types of scatter graphs. Other types of figures, such as pie charts, are less common in sport and exercise science. The following section should provide you with enough guidance to plot the most appropriate and effective figures and should help answer the common question of 'What graph should I use and when?'

4.2.1 Key considerations for plotting data

There are a number of key points that will be of help when graphing your data.

1. Figures generally plot mean data with some form of dispersion value, such as the standard deviation (SD) or standard error of the mean (SEM). Individual data is seldom plotted except for correlation analysis (which uses paired data), some performance data, individual results for an athlete report or laboratory reports when it is not possible to collect data from more than one person.
2. Data that is presented graphically is not usually concurrently presented in tables. Doing this simply duplicates the information which is presented.
3. If you have a large number of variables and are not sure which to plot, data that shows statistically significant responses and relates to your specific research question, and that you are likely to discuss the most, is probably the best bet. As a rule of thumb it is useful to present the most exciting or significant findings visually and use tables for more routine data. If you plot a basic figure for each of your variables on your spreadsheet you can easily visualise what has happened to each variable. This will help you decide which are most appropriate to plot and also may give you an indication of which data may be significant.

Now complete Exercise 4.1 to test your understanding of the different types of data presentation.

Exercise 4.1: What type of figure should I plot?

Consider the following sets of data. What type of figure would be most appropriate to display the key findings? The answers are given in Appendix 3A.

Data set	Potential figure
Relationship between personality score and performance anxiety	....
Differences between centre of gravity at heel strike during running in elite and novice runners	....
Difference in peak power during a Wingate Anaerobic test in a group of cyclists before and after 8 weeks of sprint training	....
Maximal oxygen uptake in a group of runners during two different exercise protocols	....
Motivation to train in international male rowers, national-level female rowers and club-level rowers	....
Blood pH at rest and during interval training	....
Core temperature at rest and during prolonged exercise on two occasions, one where participants could drink and one where they could not	....

4.2.2 Block graphs

Block graphs are useful when you have data that compares variables represented by one value or in one instance rather than responses over time, such as performance measures (e.g. maximal oxygen uptake, peak power output, etc). For example, if you were interested in peak power output during a sprint test in a group of endurance trained athletes and games players a block graph would be useful (see Figure 4.1). Further examples could be the maximal oxygen uptake ($\dot{V}O_{2max}$) scores during treadmill running, cycling and arm cranking in triathletes (see Figure 4.2) or pre-competition

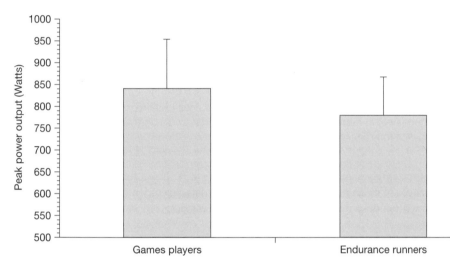

Figure 4.1 Peak power output for games players and endurance trained runners during treadmill running
Source: data from Hamilton *et al.* (1991)

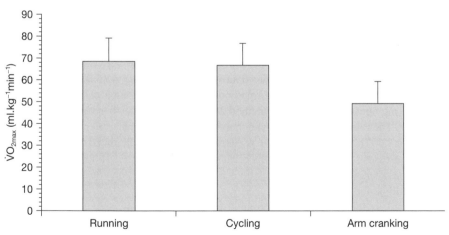

Figure 4.2 Maximal oxygen uptake ($\dot{V}O_{2max}$) for triathletes during treadmill running, cycle ergometry and arm crank ergometry
Source: data from O'Toole *et al.* (1987)

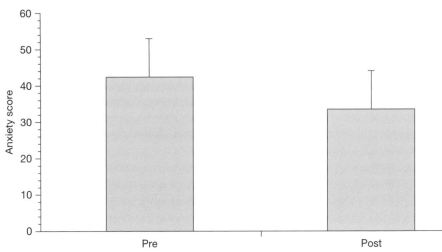

Figure 4.3 Pre- and post-competition anxiety scores (Speilberger trait questionnaire) in male runners
Source: data from Sanderson and Reilly (1983)

and post-anxiety scores in male runners (Figure 4.3). These figures clearly show the differences in mean responses. Presenting such data visually rather than as a sentence in the written description can have much more impact.

4.2.3 Scatter plots

Scatter plots have a number of uses and tend to represent more dynamic data rather than descriptive data. The most common uses of scatter plots are for correlation analysis when there are paired data (see Section 4.4.1) and for displaying data series over time. The following sections will cover both types of figure in more detail. It will also be useful to consider the corresponding sections on statistical tests in conjunction with the use of figures.

4.2.3.i Figures showing relationships

The figures for correlation data (i.e. showing a relationship between variables) are quite straightforward. Consider the data provided in Table 4.1. This data shows energy intake measured using two methods. Method 1 involved calculating energy intake using nutritional tables and method 2 involved computer-based dietary analysis software. The relationship between each method is plotted as a scatter plot and shown in Figure 4.4. The figure shows that as energy expenditure calculated from nutritional tables increases so does that from the dietary analysis software. (If both measurement techniques were valid and all calculations accurately undertaken you would hope that this would be the case.)

As well as the r^2 value it is possible to add a trend line onto your figure and the equation of the trend line. The latter is useful for predicting one response from another. In brief, the r^2 value represents the amount of variation in one variable explained by the other variable (Thomas and Nelson, 2001). The greater the r^2 value

Table 4.1 Energy intake calculated by hand from nutritional tables and from dietary analysis software

Participant	Gender	Method 1 (Kcal)	Method 2 (Kcal)
1	Female	2753	2802
2	Female	3589	2297
3	Female	3761	2528
4	Female	2368	1924
5	Female	1996	1713
6	Female	2641	2382
7	Female	2615	2262
8	Female	2849	2217
9	Female	1361	1815
10	Female	3541	3855
11	Female	1166	1231
12	Female	1885	2019
13	Female	1273	910
14	Female	1336	1185
15	Female	1101	1531
16	Female	2912	2212
17	Female	2673	2437
18	Female	2742	2064
19	Male	2311	2723
20	Male	3831	3107
21	Male	4657	4668
22	Male	4601	3902
23	Male	2515	1603
24	Male	1198	1126
25	Male	4760	3552
26	Male	3521	2142
27	Male	3487	4150
28	Male	1327	1408
29	Male	3874	3810
30	Male	2557	1979
31	Male	1988	2050
32	Male	3679	3146
33	Male	3120	2530
34	Male	2569	2298
35	Male	3609	2104
36	Male	2742	2213
37	Male	3516	1942

the better, as more variation is explained by one or other of the variables chosen. The r^2 value also helps to determine which type of trend line should be fitted to the data. Some data sets may be better suited to a curvilinear trend line rather than a linear one. If you are unsure which type of line to fit, consider which has the greatest r^2 to aid your decision.

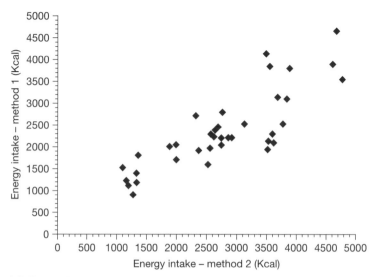

Figure 4.4 Energy intake calculated using two different methods

When using scatter plots you can also plot two different groups' data on one figure. For example, in our energy expenditure data we have data for both male and female participants and you may wish to distinguish between them. This can be done by setting out the data in your spreadsheet as shown in Table 4.2. In Microsoft Excel if you highlight both the column headings on the top row (i.e. Method 1, Male; Female) and the corresponding data below you can produce the same figure but with male and female data indicated by different symbols (see Figure 4.5). With this approach you

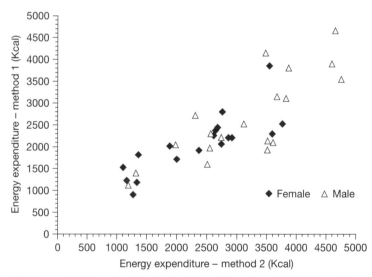

Figure 4.5 Energy intake calculated using two different methods for males and females

Table 4.2 Energy intake (Kcal) calculated by hand from nutritional tables and from dietary analysis software for males and females

Participant	Gender	Method 1	Method 2 (Kcal) Female	Method 2 (Kcal) Male
1	Female	2753	2802	
2	Female	3589	2297	
3	Female	3761	2528	
4	Female	2368	1924	
5	Female	1996	1713	
6	Female	2641	2382	
7	Female	2615	2262	
8	Female	2849	2217	
9	Female	1361	1815	
10	Female	3541	3855	
11	Female	1166	1231	
12	Female	1885	2019	
13	Female	1273	910	
14	Female	1336	1185	
15	Female	1101	1531	
16	Female	2912	2212	
17	Female	2673	2437	
18	Female	2742	2064	
19	Male	2311		2723
20	Male	3831		3107
21	Male	4657		4668
22	Male	4601		3902
23	Male	2515		1603
24	Male	1198		1126
25	Male	4760		3552
26	Male	3521		2142
27	Male	3487		4150
28	Male	1327		1408
29	Male	3874		3810
30	Male	2557		1979
31	Male	1988		2050
32	Male	3679		3146
33	Male	3120		2530
34	Male	2569		2298
35	Male	3609		2104
36	Male	2742		2213
37	Male	3516		1942

can also obtain a trend line for each group of participants. This is useful as both groups may share the same trend line (which is an important finding) or produce different trend lines (which is also an important finding).

Combining a scatter plot with correlation data is useful when comparing the relationship between variables and is particularly useful in determining the reliability or repeatability of measures (e.g. $\dot{V}O_{2max}$ from an incremental exercise protocol) as well as for assessing the validity of measures (e.g. anxiety questionaire scores vs. heart rate, or body fat percentage calculated from skinfold measure vs. hydrostatic weighing). For example, if an established exercise protocol for maximal oxygen uptake resulted in a large value you would hope that any new or alternative protocol developed would also produce a large value. This would demonstrate that those participants performing well on one test also performed well on subsequent tests. In addition, you could compare a subjective scale (such as anxiety rating) with a quantifiable physiological response (such as heart rate) to see if they are proportional to one another.

4.2.3.ii Figures showing data over time

A large number of variables, especially in physiology and biomechanics, are measured at regular or varying intervals over time. For example, metabolic variables such as blood lactate or oxygen consumption during prolonged exercise or joint angles during a specified activity, such as gait analysis or during a javelin run up. Scatter plots can be used here and it is common practice to join the data points together with straight lines. Straight lines are used as we haven't recorded any data in between the chosen time points so we don't actually know what has happened there (although it may appear obvious). Such figures differ from scatter plots for correlation analysis due to the fact that they join the data points together in series. Similar types of figures can also be plotted as line graphs. However, it is important to note that differences exist between scatter plots joined with straight lines and line graphs. The key point is that scatter plots enable data to be plotted with meaningful time intervals. With line graphs, the axis represents a set of labels rather than a continuous time scale. For example, consider Figure 4.6, where heart rate data from two trials of prolonged exercise with and without fluid replacement was recorded at 5, 15, 30, 45, and 60 min. Plotting as a scatter plot enables meaningful distances between time points to be illustrated. In Figure 4.6 you can see how the differences in time are presented between the two types of graph. Although subtle, the scatter plot approach provides a better representation of the time scale.

Another useful point to note regarding plotting line graphs relates to the data labels in the column headings of your spreadsheet. When using Microsoft Excel, if columns are labelled as anything other than a number a standard time scale will not be plotted. Subsequently replacing your column label with a number will usually automatically change your figure. Where you have data recorded during recovery from exercise as well as during exercise or during separate exercise bouts or periods of a match you will have to be careful how you label different parts of exercise protocols. For example, if you have 30 minutes of recovery data as well as 30 minutes of exercise it is best to have recovery data labelled as 35, 40, 45 min, etc. rather than have two sets of 5, 10, 15 min, etc. If you plot data with repeated timings you will soon see how differently the figure looks (Figure 4.7). A continuous time scale is generally always best.

Line graphs are useful when the important factor does not have to be time based (i.e. in minutes) or represents regular phases or intervals. In coaching, for example, expressing the volume or intensity of training each month over a one-year cycle

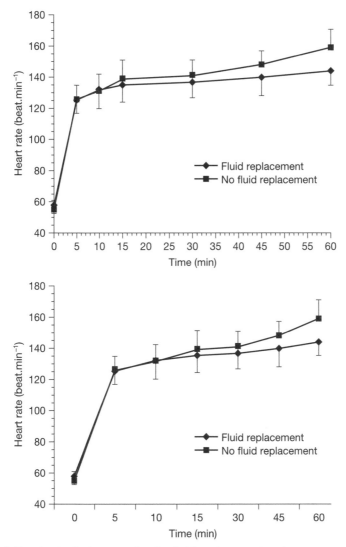

Figure 4.6 Heart rate during exercise for fluid replacement and
non-fluid-replacement trials. Data plotted as a scatter plot (top) and
as a line graph (bottom)

adapts very nicely to written labels rather than an interval scale (Figure 4.8). Here the
focus is on the month label. A variation on figures being plotted over time is when
showing data in relation to exercise intensity. This reflects how data from many incremental exercise tests is presented, the classic example being lactate threshold or
oxygen uptake (Figure 4.9).

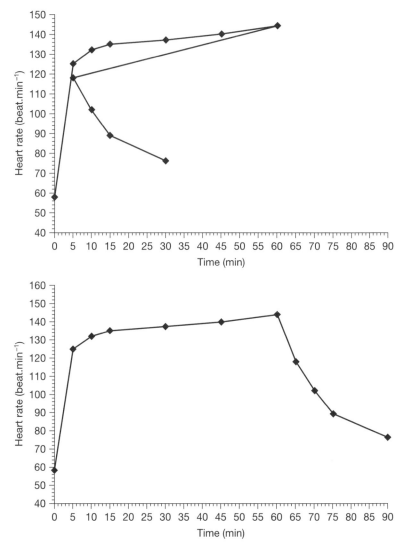

Figure 4.7 Heart rate during exercise and recovery. Plotted using non-continuous (top) and continuous (bottom) time scales

Exercise 4.2: Formatting your figures

How would you format your figures? Would you keep the figure that is automatically provided by your software or change it in any way? Consider the means and standard deviations for the data sets given in Tables 4.3–4.5. Plot the data in your usual way and then consider the points in Section 4.2.4 regarding formatting figures.

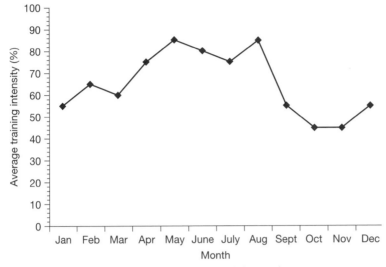

Figure 4.8 Exercise intensity over a 12-month training cycle

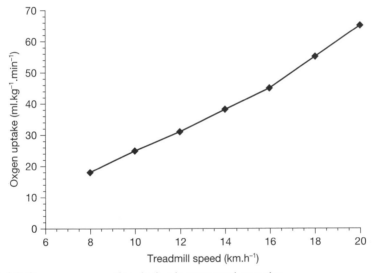

Figure 4.9 Oxygen consumption during incremental exercise

Table 4.3 Time to exhaustion at 70% $\dot{V}O_{2max}$ (data from Fallowfield et al., 1996)

		No fluid	Fluid
Time to exhaustion	Mean	77.7	103.0
	± SD	7.7	12.4

Table 4.4 Ratings of perceived exertion during prolonged exercise in cool and hot conditions (hypothetical data)

			Time (min)		
		5	15	30	60
Cool	Mean	12.0	14.0	15.0	15.0
	± SD	± 0.5	± 0.6	± 0.8	± 0.4
Heat	Mean	12.0	15.0	17.0	18.0
	± SD	± 0.4	± 0.7	± 0.6	± 0.5

Table 4.5 Exercise intensity per month over a one-year training cycle (hypothetical data)

	Intensity (%)		Intensity (%)
Jan	40	July	85
Feb	50	Aug	80
Mar	55	Sept	90
Apr	75	Oct	60
May	90	Nov	50
June	80	Dec	50

4.2.4 Formatting figures

Although there is no right or wrong way to format a figure the important thing is to be clear and consistent. The following points will help you to produce consistent scientific figures. These suggestions will not change the figure (only different data can do this) but should make it more appealing and help to get the point across visually.

4.2.4.i Titles

The title should be meaningful and describe what is happening in the figure. Avoid using phrases such as 'A graph to show . . .'. The conventional approach is to use a format similar to 'Figure 1. Ratings of perceived exertion during exercise with and without music'. Figure titles should be placed underneath the figure (but on top of tables). Some packages will automatically insert a title box for you to fill out. There is nothing stopping you from moving this text box to the bottom of the figure or simply deleting it. You can then write your own title below the figure once you have cut and pasted it into your word processing document. Try not to have duplicate titles, i.e. the automatically formatted option embedded in the figure itself and the one you have written in your main word processed document.

4.2.4.ii Axes

Axes should have a clear title (usually the variable measured and appropriate units). Axes should always have a sensible scale and represent the range of data expected, although you must consider the size of SEM or SD bars, and make sure they can be seen. If you have values in the hundreds, such as power output, it is probably best not to not start from zero. The scale should increase in regular and conventional amounts. The number of decimal places should also be considered. In calculating the mean and standard deviation most spreadsheet packages will provide a large number of values after the decimal place. It is up to you to decide what the appropriate number is. A common error is to present heart rates or power outputs in decimals. Can you have half or less of a heart beat or a Watt (considering that sport and exercise science deals with Watt values in the 100s)? As a rule of thumb you should use whatever number of decimal places the instrument or equipment measures to, although this may not always represent what is useful biologically. Consistency of decimal places is also important. Make sure that in your written description you show the same number of decimal places for the mean as you do for the SD or SEM and figure axes.

4.2.4.iii Figure size
The size of the figure and its components may initially be quite small. Arrange figures so that they are clear and do not use things such as gridlines. For example, in Microsoft Excel you can enlarge the actual graph component within the figure so that the legend is incorporated within it rather than outside of it. This makes your figures much clearer for the reader.

4.2.4.iv Legend
The legend should be clear and relate to the name of the trial undertaken or, in most instances, the condition tested rather than the variables measured. The latter is usually noted in the title. If you are printing out your work in black and white make sure that you have formatted the data markers so they can be easily distinguished from each other.

4.2.4.v Indicating significance
If you consult journal articles you will see that an asterisk (*) is commonly used to indicate significance between two points on a figure. Other symbols such as, † and φ are also commonly used for different comparisons. These can easily be added by using text boxes (see also Section 4.4, 'Using statistical tests'). A note regarding what each symbol represents can then be added to the figure legend.

4.3 Constructing tables

Annesley (2010) provides a thorough overview of how to construct tables for scientific articles. The main formatting guidelines for tables are similar to those for figures in terms of titles (but this time they go on top of the table – this is easy to remember as we put objects on the top of tables), units, decimal places, indicating significance, etc. However, if you consult author guidelines for journal articles most tables will have the following stipulations: no vertical lines; horizontal lines between the column headings and first variable; and a horizontal line at the bottom of the table. How you design your table is up to you and will depend on the data collected. Different examples are shown below for guidance (Tables 4.6 and 4.7).

Table 4.6 Example table for participants' physiological characteristics

Characteristic	Mean ± SD
Age (years)	19.2 ± 2.4
Height (m)	1.73 ± 0.07
Body mass (kg)	81.3 ± 5.6
Body fat (%)	15.3 ± 7.5
Training sessions per week	2.5 ± 1.3

Table 4.7 Example table for mean ± SD heart rate and pH data from high intensity interval training (HIT) and continuous exercise training (CET) sessions

		\multicolumn{6}{c}{Time (min)}					
		0	2	4	6	8	16
Heart rate	HIT	57 ± 8	107 ± 9	171 ± 7	116 ± 11	173 ± 12	108 ± 10
(beats.min^{-1})	CET	60 ± 6	135 ± 11	139 ± 9	139 ± 12	138 ± 9	140 ± 13
pH	HIT	7.40 ± 0.02		7.37 ± 0.03		7.34 ± 0.03	7.29 ± 0.02
	CET	7.41 ± 0.02		7.37 ± 0.04		7.39 ± 0.02	7.40 ± 0.04

Exercise 4.3: Plotting figures and tables

Using the data presented for each of the typical sport and exercise lab class examples (Appendix 1) consider how you could present the data. You should consider the key responses within the data, the type of figure used, the format of the axes and the other factors outlined in Section 4.2.4.

4.4 Using statistical tests

Before starting this section you may find it helpful to complete Exercise 4.4 to review your understanding of statistics and Exercise 4.5 to determine the statistics to be used for your own project.

Exercise 4.4: Which statistical test to use?

For the experimental designs presented below determine which statistical test or tests you could undertake to effectively analyse the data. You may find it useful to repeat this activity once you have read the next section on reporting statistics. The answers are shown in Appendix 3B.

Data set	Potential test
Relationship between personality score and performance anxiety	....
Differences between centre of gravity at heel strike during running in elite and novice runners	....
Difference in peak power during a Wingate Anaerobic test in a group of cyclists before and after 8 weeks of sprint training	....
Maximal oxygen uptake in a group of runners during two different exercise protocols	....
Motivation to train in international rowers, national-level rowers and club-level rowers	....
Blood pH at rest and during interval training	....
Core temperature at rest and during prolonged exercise on two occasions, one where participants were allowed to drink and one where they were not	....

Exercise 4.5: Determine the analysis for your pending report

For your pending laboratory report or project consult the marking scheme or criteria, course-work guidelines or laboratory schedule provided by your tutors and use the heading below to help you determine what data you have in relation to the aims of the report. Are you likely to be determining a difference or relationship? Determine the type of statistical analysis you will need to undertake.

Data set or variable	Test required
....	....
....	....
....	....
....	....
....	....
....	....
....	....

4.4.1 Correlation

Correlation determines the relationship between two variables and can be univariate or bivariate. For example, univariate correlation analyses the relationship between data for one variable recorded on two occasions, such as motivation scores from two different assessment tools. Bivariate correlation analyses the relationship between two variables, such as perception of effort and heart rate during exercise. In this instance variables don't necessarily have to have the same units but each participant has to have two (paired) data points.

4.4.1.i Main output from correlation

The key parameter you will obtain from your correlation output is the 'r' value. Table 4.8 shows a typical output from a correlation analysis involving two variables (pre-competition anxiety score from a 0–10 scale vs. introversion score on a scale of 0–100%). If you have more than one variable (e.g. ratings of perceived exertion, heart rate, blood lactate, oxygen consumption, pH) and there are a number of correlations that you are interested in you can often obtain the r values from a correlation matrix (Table 4.9). This enables you to see how all the variables you are interested in are related to each other. However, with such a blanket approach there may be a number of relationships that do not make sense (e.g. heart rate vs. pH) or a number that will always provide good relationships as they are derived from similar source data (e.g. absolute vs. relative $\dot{V}O_{2max}$ values, or body mass vs. body mass index). You will need to consider which relationships are of importance in answering your research question.

4.4.1.ii Describing results from correlations

In reporting the results of correlations there are two factors to consider. First, you can describe whether the correlation is 'low', 'moderate' or 'high'. Vincent (1999) notes that as a general rule correlation values between 0.5 to 0.7 are considered low, between 0.7 to 0.8 are considered moderate and over 0.9 are considered high. More importantly, you can determine whether the correlation is significant. It is good practice to report both the correlation coefficient and significance. However, as long as both are reported the reader can determine for themselves whether a correlation is small, medium or large. Furthermore, it is becoming more common for authors to report the actual P value rather than simply 'P < 0.05' or 'P > 0.05' for all statistical tests.

Table 4.8 Output table from a typical correlation test undertaken in Microsoft Excel

	Anxiety score	*% Introvert*
Anxiety score	1	
% Introvert	0.97338	1

Table 4.9 Correlation matrix for more than two variables from Microsoft Excel

	RPE	*Heart rate*	*Blood lactate*	*Oxygen consumption*	*pH*
RPE	1				
Heart rate	0.972044	1			
Blood lactate	0.958478	0.95144	1		
Oxygen consumption	0.947041	0.938334	0.893833	1	
pH	−0.79249	−0.7352	−0.77018	−0.61832	1

(Note: variables are still considered in pairs when the analysis of more than two variables is done at once. If you want to compare all variables together you should seek help on multiple regression techniques)

To determine the significance of a correlation you can obtain the P value directly from the given statistical output (such as correlation in SPSS or via linear regression in Excel) or look up the r values required to achieve significance from statistical tables. For the latter you will require the degrees of freedom (usually n − 2 as the data is paired) and the desired level of significance (i.e. $P < 0.05$ or $P < 0.01$). Most research methods and statistics textbooks provide such tables and are relatively easy to use. From these tables you will notice that as the number of data pairs increases (i.e. a greater number of participants) the correlation required for significance decreases. Conversely, if you desire a greater level of significance (e.g. $P < 0.01$ rather than $P < 0.05$) the r value required is also greater.

A final way to determine the strength of a relationship is using the r^2 value, as mentioned earlier in the section on scatter plots (Section 4.2.3). This is simply the r value multiplied by itself and indicates the amount of variation in one variable explained by the other variable (for further explanation see any research methods or statistics textbook). A correlation of $r = 0.97$ provides an r^2 of 0.94 (meaning 94% of the variation is accounted for, 6% is unaccounted for), whereas a correlation of $r = 0.62$ provides an r^2 of 0.38. Here there is much weaker relationship with a lot more of the variation between variables being unaccounted for.

4.4.1.iii Describing the results of correlation analysis

From the correlation table above (Table 4.8) you can see that the correlation is large. The relationship between variables also turns out to be significant. Complete Exercise 4.6 by describing the correlation.

Exercise 4.6: Describing correlation results

Describe the results from the correlation outputs provided above. You should consider reporting the size of the r value, whether it is statistically significant and the direction of the relationship (i.e. does one value increase as the other decreases?). Use mean and standard deviation values in your description. Written examples are provided in Appendix 3C.

Description: ....

....

....

....

4.4.2 T-tests

T-tests are used to determine the difference between the means of two values. These may be for the same participants undertaking the same tests on two occasions (e.g. electromyography activity during a maximal dead lift before and after a period of weight training), different participants performing the same tests (e.g. motivation to train in elite and non-elite athletes) or comparing a group's score to an established criterion or standard (e.g. cholesterol measurements in a group of athletes compared to national averages). These examples represent the use of paired (dependent) t-tests, unpaired (independent) t-tests and differences between a sample and population mean, respectively. The first two tests are much more common than the last.

4.4.2.i Main output from t-tests

The key parameter you will obtain from your t-test output is the 't' value and its associated significance (P value). The majority of studies simply report whether the difference between variables was significant, i.e. was the value less than or equal to $P = 0.05$? You do not have to report the whole results table. Look at any journal article that has used a t-test analysis and observe how the authors have presented their data. An example t-test output from Excel is shown in Table 4.10. These results are obtained from a hypothetical study examining motivation to train in elite and non-elite athletes. A 'Motivation to train questionaire' was completed by each athlete. The questionnaire produced values between 0 and 25, with higher values representing greater motivation.

Within the results table for t-tests you will usually have significance values for both one-tailed and two-tailed tests. If you already know, from your literature review and hypothesis, the likely direction of the comparison then you should concentrate on the one-tailed value. For example, maximal strength in elite weightlifters compared to non-elite. If you do not know the possible direction, such as pre-match anxiety levels in male and female hockey players, then concentrate on the two-tailed result. For our example we could assume that elite athletes would be more motivated to train – although this may not always be the case!

4.4.2.ii Describing results from t-tests

Table 4.10 shows a typical t-test output from Microsoft Excel for the example of motivation to train in elite and non-elite athletes. The resultant t statistic is shown as $t = 5.95$. If you are checking significance by using statistical tables this value would

Table 4.10 Example t-test output from Excel (using the two-sample assuming equal variances option). The output is shown as it would appear in Excel

t-test: two-sample assuming equal variances

	Elite	Non-elite
Mean	20.2	12.1
Variance	5.733333	12.76667
Observations	10	10
Pooled variance	9.25	
Hypothesised mean Difference	0	
df	18	
t stat	5.955238	
P(T<=t) one-tail	6.18E-06	
t critical one-tail	1.734064	
P(T<=t) two-tail	1.24E-05	
t critical two-tail	2.100922	

All you need to know for this output is that the difference between both one- and two-tailed tests is significant have to be equal to or greater than the critical value within the tables for it to be significant (i.e. 1.73 for a one-tailed test and 2.10 for a two-tailed test at the $P < 0.05$ level of significance). As our value is greater than the critical value our means are statistically significantly. However, the table shows the actual P values for both one-tailed (P = 6.18E-06) and two-tailed (P = 1.24E-05) tests so you don't have to consult any further statistical tables. In Table 4.10 the P values are expressed to the power of E-06 and E-05. This format is mathematical shorthand and indicates the number of zeros following the decimal point before you get to '124' for the one-tailed test or '618' for the two-tailed test. In other words $P = 0.00000618$ and $P = 0.0000124$, respectively. The use of 'E' means that the output does not have to show all the zeros – if a response is highly significant there can be quite a lot of these. Generally, if the result is reported as 'E-' it is likely to be significant. Other statistical software, such as PASW (previously SPSS), may just show $P = 0.000$. Table 4.10 also shows the degrees of freedom (df) for the test. When describing t-test results you may see the actual t value provided along with the degrees of freedom (df) in brackets such as '$t_{(18)} = 5.95$ ' for the example shown in Table 4.10.

From the t-test outputs in Table 4.10 you can see that both the one- and two-tailed comparisons are significant. Complete Exercise 4.7 by describing the t-test results.

Exercise 4.7: Describing t-tests results

Describe the results from the t-test output provided above. You should consider reporting whether the P value (and t value if appropriate for your study area) is statistically significant. If the result is significant, state which variable is greater/smaller, depending on the research question. Please note that reporting greater motivation to train in the elite or lower motivation in non-elite athletes is essentially the same result, so try not to duplicate the findings. Use mean and standard deviation values in your description. Written examples are provided in Appendix 3C.

Description: ....

....

....

....

....

....

4.4.3 Combination of correlation and t-test analysis

For some data sets it is useful to undertake both correlation and t-test analyses (pro-viding you have paired data). This is particularly so for examining how repeatable responses are. For postgraduate students it is good practice to know the repeatability of each exercise test or measure that you use. We have already used the example of $\dot{V}O_{2max}$ values being produced from an established exercise protocol and a new exercise protocol (Section 4.2.3.i). Here, you would hope that when tested twice using the same test, on separate days with sufficient recovery between tests, that similar values would be achieved. You would expect those participants who performed well on the first trial to also perform well on the second trial (giving a high correlation, Figure 4.10,

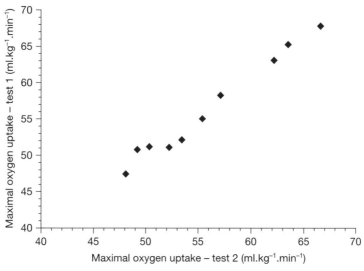

Figure 4.10 Maximal oxygen uptake during two exercise protocols

Table 4.11 t-test output from Microsoft Excel for maximal oxygen uptake during exercise on two separate occasions. The two-tailed significance is considered here (bold row) as we are not sure which test value would be correct

t-test: two-sample assuming equal variances

	Test 1	Test 2
Mean	55.77	56.24
Variance	40.62233	49.16044
Observations	10	10
Pooled variance	44.89139	
Hypothesised mean Difference	0	
df	18	
t stat	−0.15686	
P(T ≤ t) one-tail	0.438552	
t critical one-tail	1.734064	
P(T ≤ t) two-tail	**0.877104**	
t critical two-tail	2.100922	

$r = 0.989$; $P < 0.05$) with no difference between the values (as determined from a t-test, see Table 4.11). If you are interested in the repeatability of test data you should research techniques such as Limits of Agreement (Bland and Altman, 1986, 1995).

In reporting the results you could state the following:

There was no difference between trials for $\dot{V}O_{2max}$ ($P < 0.05$) and a significant correlation observed between trials ($P < 0.05$).

Alternatively you could write:

There was no difference between trials for $\dot{V}O_{2max}$ ($t_{(18)} = -0.15$; $P < 0.05$) with a significant correlation observed between trials ($r = 0.989$; $P < 0.05$).

Exercise 4.8: Combining difference and relationship analysis

Consult a range of journal articles that examine the reliability or validity of the procedures involved in your project. These studies will potentially have used both t-test and correlation analyses. For each study complete Table 4.12. Include enough detail within the 'Main aim' column so that you can see why the authors have used the given statistical test. In the 'Written description' column comment on how the authors have reported their data.

Table 4.12 Summary of study results combining difference and relationship analysis

Statistical test used	Authors	Main aim	Written description
t-test	....	....	....
			....
			....
			....
Correlation	....	....	....
			....
			....
			....
t-test and correlation combined	....	....	....
			....
			....
			....

4.4.4 Analysis of Variance (one-way analysis of variance)

Most students are confident with the use and reporting of correlations and t-tests. It is after this point when the analysis gets more complex that many students feel a little bemused, such as with analysis of variance. Analysis of variance (ANOVA) is an extension of the t-test but this time the key value is the F ratio and its associated significance. Let's first review when to use ANOVA.

The first aspect of ANOVA that often confuses students is when to use it. Consider the number of comparisons that you have. For example, if we were interested in the long jump distance (dependent variable) of different groups of athletes, and there were just two groups of athletes (e.g. elite vs. non-elite), then there would be only two sets of data and you would probably use a t-test. If you had a scenario where there was the possibility of using more than one t-test (e.g. long jump distance in three groups of athletes (e.g. under-19, under-21 and senior athletes) resulting in three possible comparisons (i.e. under-19 vs. under-21; under-19 vs. seniors; under-21 vs. seniors) then one-way ANOVA would be required. The number of 'ways' relates to the number of factors involved in the analysis. For one-way ANOVA there is only one key factor affecting the variable. In our example for the analysis of the under-19, under-21 and senior athlete long jump data the 'way' would be age and there are three different levels of it. If we took this analysis further and were interested in the same age groups but had long jump distances for both male and female athletes this would give us a second 'way' (i.e. gender). Here we would subsequently use two-way ANOVA (Section 4.4.5).

There are a number of different approaches for ANOVA and the options differ with the research design, the software that is used and the preference of the user. A good description of PASW (SPSS) procedures including different types of ANOVA is given by Ntoumadis (2001). For Microsoft Excel users there is only one option for one-way analysis of variance. However, both software packages will provide you with a sound analysis and you should decide in conjunction with advice from your tutors what the most appropriate test is for your data.

4.4.4.i Main output from one-way ANOVA

In order to consider a typical ANOVA analysis output we will continue with the example of the long jumpers used above. The data set for analysis is shown in Table 4.13 with the resulting output for Excel shown in Table 4.14 and SPSS, using one-way analysis via the general linear model, univariate analysis, shown in Table 4.15. The main value of interest is the F ratio and the accompanying P value. Both results tables show a significant F ratio ($P < 0.05$). This tells us that there is a difference somewhere between the sets of data. However, as there are three possible comparisons (i.e. under-19 vs. under-21; under-21 vs. senior; under-19 vs. senior) we don't yet know where the specific difference or differences actually are. This is where post hoc testing is important (Section 4.4.4.ii). Selecting one of the post hoc options in SPSS will enable you to find where the differences are (Table 4.16). Excel, however, does not have a post hoc option so you would have to do this manually (see Vincent, 1999).

4.4.4.ii Post hoc testing

Post hoc testing enables you to determine where differences exist in data sets containing multiple comparisons (e.g. one-way and two-way ANOVA). There are two

Table 4.13 Long jump data set for one-way analysis of variance for under-19 years (U19), under-21 years (U21) and senior athlete age groups

	Long jump distance (m)	
U19	*U21*	*Senior*
7.28	7.21	7.98
7.37	7.31	7.82
7.25	7.48	7.75
7.55	7.29	7.56
7.08	7.65	7.46
7.51	7.55	7.58
7.33	7.65	7.77
7.05	7.59	7.90

Table 4.14 One-way ANOVA statistical output for Excel. The output is shown as it would appear in Excel

ANOVA: single factor

SUMMARY

Groups	Count	Sum	Average	Variance
U19	8	58.42	7.3025	0.032307
U21	8	59.73	7.46625	0.03017
Senior	8	61.82	7.7275	0.03225

P value is less than 0.05

ANOVA

Source of variation	SS	df	MS	F	P-value	F crit
Between groups	0.735175	2	0.367588	11.64151	0.000396	3.4668
Within groups	0.663088	21	0.031576			
Total	1.398263	23				

Table 4.15 One-way ANOVA output (via general linear model) for SPSS. The output is shown as it would appear in SPSS

Tests of between-subjects effects

Dependent variable: jumpdistance

Source	Type III sum of squares	df	Mean square	F	Sig.
Corrected model	0.735*	2	0.368	11.642	0.000
Intercept	1349.550	1	1349.550	42740.288	0.000
Group	0.735	2	0.368	11.642	0.000
Error	0.663	21	0.032		
Total	1350.948	24			
Corrected total	1.398	23			

*r squared = 0.526 (adjusted r squared = 0.481)

P value for group is less than 0.05

approaches to this. The first is where the analysis software calculates the significance between various comparisons and displays the actual P value (e.g. Minitab, Statistica, some aspects of PASW). The second is where you calculate the difference required between two means for it to be significant. Vincent (1999) explains how to undertake post hoc testing manually. Here, examples for using the Tukey and Scheffé post hoc procedures are provided. If calculating by hand you are essentially determining the difference required between two means for the difference to be significant. For the long jump example, let us consider that we require a difference between group means of 0.22 m or greater for the difference to be significant. The mean long jump distances for the under-19, under-21 and senior athletes are 7.30 ± 0.18, 7.47 ± 0.17 and 7.73 ± 0.18 m. Therefore, calculating the differences between means for each group we can see that

Table 4.16 Post hoc output from SPSS (via general linear model) for long jump distance in the three groups (dependent variable labelled as 'jumpdistance', independent variable labelled as 'group' containing U19, U21 and senior (SEN) athletes). The output is shown as it would appear in SPSS

Multiple comparisons

Jumpdistance
Tukey HSD

(I)	(J)	Mean difference			95% confidence interval	
Group	Group	(I–J)	Std. error	Sig.	Lower bound	Upper bound
SEN	U19	0.4250*	0.08885	0.000	0.2011	0.6489
	U21	0.2613*	0.08885	0.020	0.0373	0.4852
U19	SEN	−0.4250*	0.08885	0.000	−0.6489	−0.2011
	U21	−0.1638	0.08885	0.180	−0.3877	0.0602
U21	SEN	−0.2613*	0.08885	0.020	−0.4852	−0.0373
	U19	0.1638	0.08885	0.180	−0.0602	0.3877

Based on observed means
The error term is mean square (error) = 0.032
*The mean difference is significant at the 0.05 level

P values are less than 0.05

P values not less than 0.05

the difference between under-19 and under-21 groups (7.30 m − 7.47 m = 0.17 m) is not significant. However, the difference between the under-19 and senior athletes is significant (7.30 m − 7.73 m = 0.43 m) and so to is the difference between the under-21 and senior athletes (7.47 m − 7.73 m = 0.26 m). You can annotate such significance on any figure that you may produce. An example of the SPSS post hoc output for this example is shown in Table 4.16.

4.4.4.iii Describing results from one-way ANOVA
For the results of ANOVA tests it is a good habit to report the overall result and then any post hoc testing if appropriate. As with t-tests you may see the F ratio itself reported with the accompanying degrees of freedom for the between groups and within (error) groups comparisons. For the example in Table 4.14 these are 2 and 21, respectively, which is reported as $F_{(2,21)} = 11.642$. Complete Exercise 4.9 by describing the one-way ANOVA results above.

Exercise 4.9: Describing one-way ANOVA results

Describe the results from the one-way ANOVA outputs provided above. You should consider whether there is a statistically significant result and summarise the results of any post hoc analysis. Use mean and standard deviation values in your description. Written examples are provided in Appendix 3C.

Description: ....

....

....

....

....

....

4.4.5 Analysis of variance (two-way analysis of variance)

Two-way analysis of variance is a common statistical test in sport and exercise science. As noted earlier the two 'ways' relate to the two key factors affecting your (dependent) variable of interest. For example, consider a study where you are interested in blood lactate responses during a continuous exercise training session (CON) and an interval training session (INT). We will assume that both sessions are matched for total work done and energy expenditure (e.g. as in Christmass *et al.*, 1999) with blood lactate measures taken at rest and at a number of time points throughout each session (rest, 4, 8 and 16 minutes). Here the dependent variable is the blood lactate concentration as it *depends* upon the protocol undertaken and the time at which the measurement is made. However, we are not only interested in how blood lactate concentration changes over time (one-way) and how the blood lactate differs between training types (a second way) but also how the two factors interact. In other words, how does the blood lactate response change in relation to the type of training session and time? This final comparison is called the interaction. A typical data set is shown in Table 4.17.

Table 4.17 Typical data set for two-way ANOVA

One way (comparison over time) →

	Time (min)			
	0	4	8	16
CON	1.8	5.4	4.1	3.2
	0.8	4.9	4.1	3.8
	1.5	5.1	4.7	3.1
	1.6	3.8	3.1	2.5
	1.1	4.1	3.9	2.9
	0.9	5.3	5.1	4.7
	1.2	4.9	3.9	3.2
INT	1.6	5.6	6.8	7.4
	0.9	4.9	5.6	6.9
	1.4	6.1	7.1	7.9
	1.3	4.5	5.9	7.3
	0.8	4.9	5.7	6.9
	1.3	6.1	7.2	8.1
	0.9	5.6	6.8	8.3

Second way (comparison between groups)

4.4.5.i Main output from two-way ANOVA

As with one-way analysis of variance both Excel and PASW have functions to compute various types of two-way ANOVA. The statistical output from the analysis of the blood lactate data using Excel's 'Two way ANOVA with replication' (repeated measures) and from PASW's 'General Linear Model' are shown in Tables 4.18 and 4.19, respectively. If we take the Excel output first you can see a large amount of information in the results table. The first few sections provide the number of data points and the sum, mean and variance for each variable. These are all the stages required to calculate the final F ratio (to appreciate the calculation process refer to any research methods or statistics textbook).

Table 4.18 Typical statistical output for two-way ANOVA (Excel: two-way ANOVA with replication)

Anova: two-factor with replication

SUMMARY

	0	4	8	16	Total
CON					
Count	7	7	7	7	28
Sum	8.9	33.5	28.9	23.4	94.7
Average	1.271429	4.785714	4.128571	3.342857	3.382143
Variance	0.139048	0.368095	0.405714	0.509524	2.126706
INT					
Count	7	7	7	7	28
Sum	8.2	37.7	45.1	52.8	143.8
Average	1.171429	5.385714	6.442857	7.542857	5.135714
Variance	0.092381	0.394762	0.469524	0.319524	6.319418
Total					
Count	14	14	14	14	
Sum	17.1	71.2	74	76.2	
Average	1.221429	5.085714	5.285714	5.442857	
Variance	0.109505	0.449011	1.845934	5.131868	

ANOVA

Source of variation	SS	df	MS	F	P value	F crit
Sample	43.05018	1	43.05018	127.6236	4.03E-15	4.042652
Columns	173.1234	3	57.7078	171.0766	1.26E-25	2.798061
Interaction	38.73054	3	12.91018	38.27263	8.83E-13	2.798061
Within	16.19143	48	0.337321			
Total	271.0955	55				

P values less than 0.05

Table 4.19 Typical statistical output for two-way ANOVA (using general linear model). The format of the output is shown as it would appear in SPSS

Tests of between-subjects effects

Dependent variablac: bloodlactate

Source	Type III sum of squares	df	Mean square	F	Sig.
Corrected model	254.904[†]	7	36.415	107.953	0.000
Intercept	1015.754	1	1015.754	3011.236	0.000
Group	43.050	1	43.050	127.624	0.000
Time	173.123	3	57.708	171.077	0.000
Group*Time	38.731	3	12.910	38.273	0.000
Error	16.191	48	0.337		
Total	1286.850	56			
Corrected total	271.096	55			

[†]r squared = 0.940 (adjusted r squared = 0.932)

P values less than 0.05

To begin with you only need to focus on the final section of the output which provides the F ratio and the accompanying significance values. Here you will see a line of results for each of 'Sample', 'Columns' and 'Interaction'. Before we discuss these results it is important to know the aspects of the data they represent. First consider how you have set up your data in Excel (Table 4.17). The 'Sample' refers to the two types of training (i.e. CON vs. INT). The 'Columns' relate to the time component of the data (i.e. each time point was recorded in a separate column on the spreadsheet). The 'Interaction' relates to how these two factors interact with each other. These concepts are shown in Tables 4.20a–c. As a simplified view, the 'Sample' analysis is concerned only with the responses of the continuous vs. interval training data as a whole and is effectively comparing two means (and the associated variance), one representing all the data for the CON group and one for the INT group. Therefore, this is a general group comparison and it is not concerned with the time aspects. The 'Column' analysis is concerned only with the responses over time, not with the differences between training type. Here the analysis effectively compares a mean value (and associated variance) for all the resting data, with all the 4, 8 and 16 min data across both samples. As these comparisons relate to general rather than specific responses they are referred to as *main effects*. The interaction is concerned with how the group and time factors interact specifically with each other. This is shown in Table 4.20c where the factors overlap. Here, time 0 min for CON could be compared against time 0 min for INT or time 4 min for CON or time 8 min for CON or time 16 min for CON, etc. In other words, the specific comparisons you would be interested in if you were to do multiple t-tests – which of course you wouldn't do!

In general, we are most interested in the interaction term. If this is significant we know that there is a difference somewhere in the data. You can then undertake post hoc tests to determine where the specific differences actually lie, as you would for a one-way ANOVA. If the interaction term is not significant than you can examine the

Table 4.20a Schematic representing 'Sample' concept

	Time (min)			
	0	*4*	*8*	*16*
CON	1.8	5.4	4.1	3.2
	0.8	4.9	4.1	3.8
	1.5	5.1	4.7	3.1
	1.6	3.8	3.1	2.5
	1.1	4.1	3.9	2.9
	0.9	5.3	5.1	4.7
	1.2	4.9	3.9	3.2
INT	1.6	5.6	6.8	7.4
	0.9	4.9	5.6	6.9
	1.4	6.1	7.1	7.9
	1.3	4.5	5.9	7.3
	0.8	4.9	5.7	6.9
	1.3	6.1	7.2	8.1
	0.9	5.6	6.8	8.3

Data in each sample represents all data with respect to each group (i.e. CON and INT). This represents the 'main effect' for sample and is not concerned with any other factor

Table 4.20b Schematic representing 'Columns' concept

	Time (min)			
	0	*4*	*8*	*16*
CON	1.8	5.4	4.1	3.2
	0.8	4.9	4.1	3.8
	1.5	5.1	4.7	3.1
	1.6	3.8	3.1	2.5
	1.1	4.1	3.9	2.9
	0.9	5.3	5.1	4.7
	1.2	4.9	3.9	3.2
INT	1.6	5.6	6.8	7.4
	0.9	4.9	5.6	6.9
	1.4	6.1	7.1	7.9
	1.3	4.5	5.9	7.3
	0.8	4.9	5.7	6.9
	1.3	6.1	7.2	8.1
	0.9	5.6	6.8	8.3

Data in columns represents all data with respect to time. This represents the 'main effect' for time and is not concerned with any other factor

Table 4.20c Schematic representing 'Interaction' concept

	Time (min)			
	0	*4*	*8*	*16*
CON	1.8	5.4	4.1	3.2
	0.8	4.9	4.1	3.8
	1.5	5.1	4.7	3.1
	1.6	3.8	3.1	2.5
	1.1	4.1	3.9	2.9
	0.9	5.3	5.1	4.7
	1.2	4.9	3.9	3.2
INT	1.6	5.6	6.8	7.4
	0.9	4.9	5.6	6.9
	1.4	6.1	7.1	7.9
	1.3	4.5	5.9	7.3
	0.8	4.9	5.7	6.9
	1.3	6.1	7.2	8.1
	0.9	5.6	6.8	8.3

Where the group and time shapes overlap represent the possible interactions of these factors and each set of data which can be compared against each other main effects for each factor involved in the ANOVA. These results are not as specific but can provide useful general information. The results table for the PASW analysis (Table 4.19) shows the same information as in the Excel output, although the main effects are labelled according to how you labelled the PASW data sheet columns. In this instance they are 'Group' and 'Time'. The interaction term is labelled 'Group*Time'. PASW does not easily provide post hoc data for some interactions so you will have to determine where the differences lie just as you would have to for the analysis in Excel.

4.4.5.ii Meaningful post hoc comparisons

When you have a significant interaction you can then compare any two means with each other. However, there is the possibility that you may have a large number of potential comparisons. So, which post hoc comparisons are useful to report? In some instances you may find only one or two so it is quite easy to report them. In other instances, especially if you calculate the post hoc values by hand, you will need to decide which comparisons are useful.

For example, if you had core temperature measures every 5 min over a 60 min duration of exercise and recovery for two or three different trials there would be a large number of potential comparisons. So, which means should you compare? Consider the figure for blood lactate against time relating to the example above for two different training sessions (Figure 4.11). The number of useful comparisons will usually relate to your research question. Although we may primarily be interested in whether there is a difference in blood lactate concentration between the training types at each time point it is also important to see where differences in responses begin to appear within each trial and if there are differences at the end of exercise. In the blood lactate example, the figure shows the most likely differences would be not only at the end of exercise but also where blood lactate increases during one trial but decreases in the other. Here it may be useful to be able to state whether these changes were

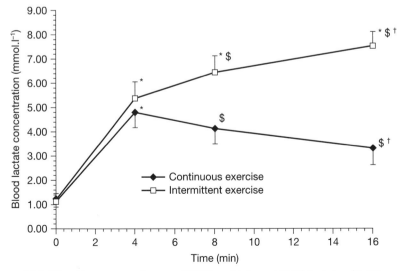

Figure 4.11 Blood lactate continuous (CON) and interval (INT) training (* different from resting values [P < 0.05]; $ different from CON at same timepoint [P < 0.05]; † different from 8 minutes [P < 0.05])

significant. Some useful comparisons to consider for most experimental designs are suggested below:

1. **Comparing resting values**. This comparison tells you if the resting data is the same. Hopefully this will be the case so each participant is in the same physiological or psychological state, unless your study design suggests otherwise. Either way it is useful to compare.
2. **Differences at given time points**. This is important to determine whether differences exist *between* trials.
3. **Changes over time in specific trials**. This is important to determine whether differences exist *within* trials. This could involve comparing values within one trial to resting values or between different time points in that trial. This comparison may reveal different trends and adaptations between trials.
4. **Differences at the end of exercise**. For many research designs this is the important comparison and will tell you if differences exist at the end of the experiment as a result of a given treatment.

4.4.5.iii Describing results for two-way ANOVA interaction

As with one-way ANOVA the first aspect that you would normally report is the overall significance. In the case of two-way ANOVA that is the interaction along with any specific comparisons from the post hoc analysis. For example, the results in Tables 4.18 and 4.19 show a significant interaction between blood lactate concentration with respect to time and with training type. From post hoc analysis we would also have determined that significant differences exist between blood lactate concentrations at the following points:

1. Between 4, 8 and 16 minutes compared to rest for both trials.
2. Between CON and INT trials at 8 and 16 minutes.
3. Between 8 and 16 minutes within both training types.

As with t-tests and one-way ANOVA you can express the results of two-way ANOVA using the F ratio and degrees of freedom as well as the P value. As you have three different results for two-way ANOVA (two main effects and the interaction) there are three different combinations of degrees of freedom to report. The format of reporting requires two degrees of freedom values. First, the value for the specific result you are reporting and second, the degrees of freedom for the error (or within) term. This second term is the same for each result. For the two-way ANOVA outputs provided in Tables 4.18 and 4.19 these would be $F_{(1,48)}$, $F_{(3,48)}$ and $F_{(3,48)}$ for the main effect for group, main effect for time and the interaction, respectively. Complete Exercise 4.10 by describing the two-way ANOVA results above.

Exercise 4.10: Describing two-way ANOVA results

Describe the results from the two-way ANOVA outputs provided above. You should consider whether there is a statistically significant interaction. If not, are there any significant main effects? Also, summarise the results of any post hoc analysis and use mean and standard deviation values in your description. A written example is provided in Appendix 3C.

Description: ....

....

....

....

....

....

4.4.5.iv Describing results for two-way ANOVA main effects

Let us consider the scenario where the results in Tables 4.18 and 4.19 did *not* give a significant interaction. In this instance we can fall back to the main effects to examine general responses. In sport and exercise science there is very often a significant main effect for the 'time' factor due to most variables being elevated with exercise (e.g. heart rate, oxygen consumption) or in some instances decreasing with exercise (e.g. blood pH and blood bicarbonate concentration), so this won't really tell us a lot. The key factor to examine here is probably the main effect for the treatment (e.g. training type or group). However, as there were only two training types that we were interested in we already know that there is a difference between them, so a post hoc analysis here won't provide any further information. Indeed, in PASW you would come across an error message in the results output stating that 'no post hoc analysis was undertaken for group as there were fewer than three groups'. This does not mean you have done anything wrong, just that the next level of analysis can't be completed as you effectively already have the answer. If we had three types of training (continuous exercise, interval training, interval training at a different intensity) we could undertake a post hoc analysis of the training types in order to find which training type provided the greatest blood lactate values – in general. However, if there was no significant interaction observed we couldn't be any more specific than that.

In the above case you could describe the data in the following way:

No interaction was observed for blood lactate concentration between time and training type ($P > 0.05$). However, a significant main effect was observed between trials ($P < 0.05$) with the interval training eliciting greater blood lactate concentration than for the continuous exercise training.

Now that you have practised writing results descriptions for each of the statistical tests covered, read the results section of previous journal articles using ANOVA techniques and complete Exercise 4.11. You can then go on to critique a range of written descriptions (Exercise 4.12) and then write the results section for your own data (Exercise 4.13).

Exercise 4.11: One-way and two-way ANOVA results

Consult a range of journal articles to find those which have used one- and two-way ANOVA analysis. For each study complete Table 4.21. Include enough detail within the 'Main aim' column so that you can see why the authors have used the given statistical test. For the 'Written description' column comment on how the authors have reported their data.

Table 4.21 One-way and two-way ANOVA results from previous research studies

Statistical test used	Authors	Main aim	Written description
One-way ANOVA	....	....	....
			....
			....
			....
Two-way ANOVA	....	....	....
			....
			....
			....

Exercise 4.12: Critiquing a written description

For the data in Table 4.22, Figure 4.12, and the statistical output in Table 4.23 comment on how the written descriptions could be improved. There are two different written descriptions to critique. The data is for a hypothetical study examining the effects of music tempo on ratings of perceived exertion during continuous exercise at 60% $\dot{V}O_{2max}$ for 30 minutes. Example comments for the descriptions are given in Appendix 3C.

Written description 1

As you can see from the graph there is an increase in RPE. One trial is higher than the other. There are differences between trials.

Comments: ....

....

....

....

....

....

Written description 2

The results are shown in the graph. RPE is similar at 5 minutes of exercise giving values of 12.3 and 13.4. At 10 minutes values go up to 12.6 and 14.3. Values then increase at 15 minutes to 13.4 and 14.9. At the end of exercise values go up to 13.9 and 15.0.

Comments: ....

....

....

....

....

....

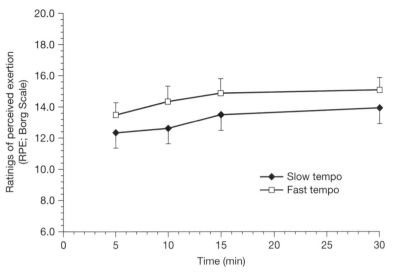

Figure 4.12 Rating of perceived exertion during continuous exercise in the presence of fast- or slow-tempo music

Table 4.22 Data set for Exercise 4.12

	Time (min)			
	5	*10*	*15*	*30*
Slow tempo	12	13	14	14
	11	12	13	14
	13	13	14	15
	14	13	14	15
	12	11	12	13
	11	13	13	12
	13	13	14	14
Fast tempo	14	15	15	15
	12	13	14	15
	14	15	16	16
	14	15	16	16
	13	13	14	14
	13	14	14	14
	14	15	15	15

Table 4.23 Statistical output for Exercise 4.12

ANOVA

Source of variation	SS	df	MS	F	P value	F crit
Sample	25.78571	1	25.78571	31.16547	1.08E-06	4.042652
Columns	21.14286	3	7.047619	8.517986	0.000122	2.798061
Interaction	0.785714	3	0.261905	0.316547	0.813332	2.798061
Within	39.71429	48	0.827381			
Total	87.42857	55				

Exercise 4.13: Producing your own written description

Using the pointers in Exercise 4.12 produce a written description for your own ANOVA data. For extra practice you could also consider writing a results section for each of the typical lab class examples used throughout this book.

Written description for your own data: ....

....

....

....

....

....

....

....

4.5 Don't be afraid of error messages!

Most statistics packages or spreadsheets with statistics options normally provide error messages if something is not quite right with the data set-up or analysis procedures. Although these are designed to help you they may seem daunting at first glance and mean little to you. However, with a little thought you can usually work out what the problem is. For example, Excel will tell you that 'Output will overwrite existing data' if the output region for the statistics analysis will cover something else already on your spreadsheet. In this instance all you have to do is to direct your output to a different cell or area on your spreadsheet or to a new spreadsheet. Also, as noted earlier, for two-way analysis of variance in SPSS you may get the message 'No post hoc results for group as fewer than three groups'. This just means that there are only two groups to compare for main effects, the results for which you would already have from your two-way ANOVA output. If you had three or more groups to compare this would not appear.

4.6 Common errors in results sections

There are a number of common errors that many students display when writing their results sections. The following are the most common to be avoided. Doing so will not only help to improve the flow of your results section but also your marks for this section.

4.6.1 Discussing results

Within your results section you should only present and describe the results. It is very common for students to try and explain or discuss their results within the results section. Try to avoid this as you have a discussion section specifically for this purpose.

4.6.2 Reporting variables not described in the methods

You need to ensure that all of the results you present have been adequately described in the methods. Conversely, you also need to ensure that all of the variables described in the methods are reported in the results. Otherwise, what was the point of measuring them? Even if variables do not result in any significant differences a single sentence may be all that is required to inform the reader of the main finding.

4.6.3 Duplicating data in tables and figures

Avoid duplicating your data by presenting results in both figure and table formats. The description of your data should be sufficient to provide the key responses and any specific values of interest.

4.6.4 Poor description of the results

Poor written descriptions do not help demonstrate the key findings of the study. Always make sure that you have reported the key statistical results and any values which aid this description. In addition, the actual statistical outputs from each test (i.e. the output tables) are seldom required in written reports. You may need these tables within your project lab file as evidence of data analysis or even as appendices (check your coursework guidance) but they are not usually contained within the results section per se. A common error is when your data may look as if it would yield a strong correlation but you have not actually undertaken a correlation analysis. Here many students state that 'there is a positive correlation' but if you have not done the analysis it is better to state that there is 'a linear relationship'.

4.6.5 Unclear reporting of statistics

If you are not confident with the statistical analysis it is likely that you will also not be confident in reporting the key findings of each test. Try to keep the message simple. Focus on stating whether the results for each test were significant in conjunction with reporting whether the P values were greater or less than 0.05. Also make sure that you have the greater than (>) and less than (<) symbols written correctly. Confusing these symbols could have important implications on your results and demonstrate a lack of understanding of statistics. It is becoming more common for authors to report the actual P value rather than simply 'P < 0.05' or 'P > 0.05'.

4.6.6 Repeating the statistical tests used

You do not have to repeat the statistical tests undertaken as this will have been described in the methods section.

4.6.7 Inconsistent reporting of values and units

As noted in the methods it is important to use the correct units for all variables and an appropriate number of decimal places. It is also important not to forget to state the standard deviation values with each mean value reported.

4.6.8 Lack of reference to figures and tables

If you have figures and tables in your report it is important to state which figure your particular description relates to (see the example written descriptions earlier in this chapter). If figures and tables are not labelled clearly the flow of the results from the perspective of the readers or assessors will be affected.

4.7 Chapter summary and reflection

This chapter considered different ways of analysing and presenting your results. Different types of figure may be more effective than others in displaying the key findings of your study. The main statistical tests for different types of research design were also considered. This chapter also considered how to write your results section through a series of exercises relating to each statistical test. To assess your understanding of results sections answer the following summary questions:

- What is the purpose of a results section?
- What are main ways of expressing your key findings?
- How do your results reflect your research question or hypothesis?
- What are the common errors when writing results sections?

4.8 Further activities

Go to the website of a journal that you regularly read or are aware of. Find the author guidelines and consider the advice given for writing results sections.

Use the critical appraisal tools in the introduction chapter to evaluate your own results section.

Consult your lab schedule and ensure that you understand the expected results for each variable you have measured.

Chapter 5

Discussion

In this chapter you will be able to:

- appreciate the purpose of the discussion (Section 5.1)
- consider the components of your discussion (section 5.2)
- plan your discussion (Section 5.3)
- practise writing part of your discussion (Section 5.4)
- consider what your results mean (Sections 5.5 and 5.6)
- appreciate the role of the conclusion (Section 5.7)
- identify limitations and future work (Section 5.8)
- reflect upon your research question and hypotheses (Section 5.9)
- identify common problems when writing discussions (Section 5.6)

5.1 Purpose of the discussion

Once the research study has been designed, and the data collected and analysed, it is time to explain what it all means. For many readers of scientific articles the discussion is often the most important section and, along with the methods, is a key section for critique (see Section 2.8). The discussion should emphasise the new and important aspects of the study without repeating information and details from other sections (ICMJE, 1997). The discussion should also compare and contrast the results to previous research studies (Foote, 2009b; ICMJE, 1997) to put the results into context and assert their value (Skelton, 1994). Importantly, the discussion should explain how the results help to answer and support the research question posed (Foote, 2009b). Finally, the discussion is also the opportunity to present your limitations and future work (ICMJE, 1997).

The guidance provided for writing your lab report discussion can take many forms. For example, in your first year of study you may have a series of questions to answer relating to your data that provide the focus required. Alternatively you may simply be asked to 'discuss your results'. The latter is certainly likely for final-year dissertations and postgraduate theses. Having written lab reports in the formative years of your studies you will be expected to already know how to approach your discussion. This chapter provides an overview of what your discussion is expected to contain and some guidance on how to plan and write it. As with previous chapters it is also useful to consult the information on the critical appraisal of journal articles (see Section 2.8) to appreciate those areas often lacking in discussion sections.

5.2 Components of your discussion

The discussion and the results section are considered to be the most difficult sections of scientific reports to write (Foote, 2009b). Indeed, the discussion is a section which often clearly discriminates between students of different abilities or grades, probably more so than other sections of the report. When written well, however, the discussion provides an excellent opportunity to achieve good marks. Therefore it is important to grasp the key factors required. So, how do you go about writing your discussion and what actually needs to be contained within it? It may seem obvious to state that this is the section where you discuss your results but what does this actually mean? The following paragraph should help to start you off prior to the 'planning your discussion' section.

Wells (2006) and Alexandrov (2004) have considered three- and four-part or 'paragraph' approaches, respectively (see Figure 5.1). Although these authors were concerned with providing guidance for writing journal articles the concept is essentially the same for both dissertations and lab reports. Wells (2006) suggests a three-part approach akin to the 'three paragraph' approach used for writing introductions. Here the first part considers the general background to the study, the second contains a brief description of the main results and the third looks at how the new results add to the field of research. Alexandrov (2004) suggests a four-part model that starts with the statement 'Our study showed . . .'. The second section notes the novelty of the findings or how they parallel previous research. In the third part there is a description of how the work contradicts previous research and the final paragraph considers the study's strengths and and limitations, and any unresolved questions, and looks towards future research. For those authors struggling to begin writing discussions for journal articles, Branson (2004) considers a more specific eight-part (or paragraph) approach (Table 5.1).

All the aspects suggested by the authors above are important to include in your discussion. However, a more straightforward approach for undergraduates is to

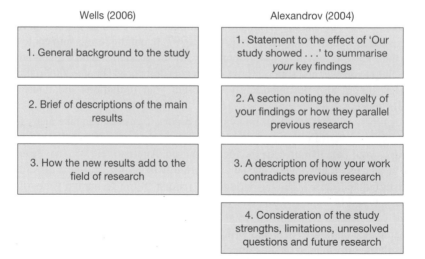

Figure 5.1 Three- and four-part models for discussions

Table 5.1 Generic construct for writing the discussion (Branson, 2004)

Paragraph	Objective
1	Describe the major findings Answer the research question Don't make conclusions
2	Interpret your findings Explain what you think the main findings mean Don't over-interpret
3–5	Compare your results with the current literature on the same or similar topics Use references to support your interpretation of your findings and the current literature Explain any literature that conflicts with your data and explain why the reports conflict
6	List the limitations of your study Describe the generalisability of your result to other situations Describe the problem you encountered in the methods
7	List unanswered questions Propose further research that should be undertaken
8	Conclusion Answer the research question and explain your interpretation of the findings Don't make conclusions unsupported by the results

consider all the variables measured within your report and think about what they mean. Try not to miss any out. As you progress through your studies your level of understanding will increase and so will the expectations of critique and explanation. Therefore, it will also be useful to consider the chapter on critical appraisal tools (see Chapter 2) and the comments relating to discussion sections. Section 5.2 will consider ways to plan your discussion and get your writing started.

Many students become concerned that they are repeating information from their literature review or introduction within their discussions. This is understandable as many of the key journal articles used may well be the same. Wells (2006) summarises the differences between introductions and discussions as follows: introductions consider what was known before the experiment was done and discussions compare the new results found in the study and integrates them with previous literature. Furthermore, the information within your lab report introduction often sets the scene for the tests to be undertaken, whereas your dissertation introduction should develop the rationale for your research question (see Chapter 1). A common question from students is 'Can I use the same references in the discussion as in the introduction?' The answer is, of course, yes you can. As your discussion is attempting to explain your lab results and answer your research question you will of course have to refer to studies cited in your introduction or literature review. The main difference is how you use the sources within your discussion. Consider Exercise 5.1 to determine how sources may be used differently in introductions and discussions.

Exercise 5.1: Distinguishing between introductions and discussions

Read the discussion of a journal article and compare it to the introduction. How does the use of information differ between them?

Key focus of the introduction: ....

....

....

....

Key focus of the discussion: ....

....

....

....

Where the authors have used the same references in both sections consider how the reference has been used. What key information is included in both sections? How is the information used different?

Reference: ....

How used in introduction: ....

....

....

....

How used in the discussion: ....

....

....

....

5.3 Planning your discussion

There are a number of ways to plan your discussion and you will no doubt find one that works best for you. As such there is no right or wrong way to do this providing all the relevant information is considered. You could simply go straight into writing without much planning and see what evolves. However, as with exams, this approach could result in you writing off topic or forgetting something that is crucial to your work. For all reports and scientific studies it is essential that you relate back to your aims and hypotheses to see if you have managed to answer your research question. As has been emphasised throughout this text in relation to other sections of your report, always have your research question in mind. The following may help you to start thinking about what the important factors are in your data:

1. With your results section or your spreadsheet of data open in front of you look at the responses for each variable you have measured. It may be helpful to produce a

(basic) figure or plot of your mean data to visualise what has happened. You can also do this prior to your statistical analysis. You can then view your responses and think about what they show. It may be helpful to add a sentence of initial thoughts as to what has happened under each figure on your spreadsheet. By doing this you will at least consider the underlying responses for each variable. Remember, everything you measured was measured for a reason.

2. Look at each group of variables that you have measured, i.e. cardiorespiratory, metabolic, perceptual, EMG, kinematic, personality, mood, performance (e.g. power, speed, agility), etc. What are the logical links between them? Do the responses complement each other? Would you expect them to? Use your answers to plan specific themes throughout your discussion.

3. Can you see a logical order or progression to the data? Do you have performance measures and some corresponding variables relating to underlying mechanisms? Do some variables lend themselves to explaining others? For example, how were different levels of anxiety provoked in your study and what were the resultant heart rate responses reflecting this?

4. Consider the subheadings you have in the method and results sections. This is a good model to follow for your discussion. You don't necessarily have to keep the subheadings in the text in your final version but it may help your planning.

5. Refer to your research question. Have you managed to answer it? Can you reject or accept your hypotheses?

Exercise 5.2: Structure of a discussion

Read the discussion section of a journal article related to your lab report or project. Choose one or two words to describe what each paragraph discusses.

Paragraph 1: ....

Paragraph 2: ....

Paragraph 3: ....

Paragraph 4: ....

Paragraph 5: ....

Paragraph 6: ....

Paragraph 7: ....

Paragraph 8: ....

Examine your list of areas covered within the journal articles discussion and examine the flow of information. Is there a logical progression? How did the discussion evolve? In what order did the authors discuss their findings?

Compare your descriptors to what is contained within the results section. Were all the results considered? How were the variables grouped within the discussion?

Now we have considered the components of a discussion and how you plan it the next stage is to actually write it.

5.4 Writing your discussion

As you may have noticed from your background reading of journal articles, across the different sport and exercise disciplines, the writing styles of authors differ considerably. If there was a magic formula to produce an ideal discussion then writing would be formulaic, but this would not allow you to add you own personal slant to explaining your data, and the result would probably be uninspiring. However, although developing your own writing style is of great importance there are number of factors that you should consider when writing your discussion. These are by no means the only way to present your discussion points, but they do attempt to provide a focus for contextualising your results.

After reading Section 5.3 relating to planning your discussion you should by now have some idea of what your data is showing in terms of its absolute values, i.e. what increased, what decreased and by how much? If you stop at this point and do not explain the responses your discussion will be descriptive and not explanatory. This is not the foundation for a good report and is likely to achieve lower marks. You need to make sure you develop your discussion. Consider the purpose of the main body of the discussion as noted in Section 5.1. The discussion should do the following:

1. Emphasise the new and important aspects.
2. Compare and contrast the results with previous research and put them into context.
3. Explain how the results help to answer the research question.

The following sections will consider each point and how you may demonstrate them.

5.4.1 Emphasise the new and important aspects

You first need to make it clear what your new findings are. This is closely related to your research question and the uniqueness of your study. If you have not examined anything 'new' then your results are likely to be more confirmatory than novel. (This is more important a consideration for postgraduate students and other researchers who want to publish their work than it is for undergraduate students.) If you have not found anything 'new' (whether statistically significant or otherwise) this is not a major problem; results that are not statistically significant are just as important as those that are significant – especially if you were expecting a considerable difference. However, it is also important not to overestimate the importance or implications of your key findings if significance is not evident.

5.4.2 Compare and contrast the results with previous research and put them into context

This second aspect is extremely important. Comparing your results to other studies helps you to contextualise your data. However, not everyone knows what 'contextualise' means. If you consult a thesaurus for variant words and phrases for 'context' you will find such entries as 'connection', 'frame of reference' and 'relation' (*Collins Shorter Thesaurus*, 1994). Therefore, contextualising your results means relating your findings to previous research studies and determining how your results fit in with the current body of knowledge. For example, are your peak power values from the Wingate anaerobic test similar to other studies examining similar populations? Are your personality profiles as expected for trained athletes? Are your ground reaction forces within the normal range? Are your $\dot{V}O_{2max}$ values lower than for elite athletes but greater then untrained participants? Here you should include a selection of the most pertinent references (Alexandrov, 2004) but not an exhaustive list of the literature. In a review of research articles, Clarke and Chalmers (1998) and Clarke *et al.* (2002) noted that although previous studies were cited within the discussion sections it was often unclear as to whether these studies represented similar study designs or why they had been included. Therefore, in general, consider referencing those studies which have used a similar population, protocol or methods to your own. If studies are used that are not similar (which may often be the only literature available) note this and explain what the differences between those studies and your own may be.

Comparison of your results to previous studies can also be used to demonstrate that your data is of good quality. For example, are your resting values or performances similar to what is expected? For undergraduate dissertations this is a good illustration of the accuracy of your data collection techniques; for postgraduate students on the other hand, a high level of accuracy would certainly be expected or presumed. Consider the example of measuring blood lactate concentration in midfielders and defenders during a simulated soccer match. You may not have found significant differences between your groups but were the overall values within the expected range? Discussing this aspect demonstrates your knowledge of the general responses to a simulated soccer match, which is as important at many levels of study. A discussion of such responses also helps to validate your data. Likewise, you may not have observed any performance differences in basketball shooting ability in high- and low-anxiety conditions but was the performance of the players as good as expected for their level of experience or the test used? This may lead you on to reasons why accuracy may differ between studies, thus initiating thoughts of study limitations and stimulating future research ideas. For example, if we had found no difference in shooting performance between the expert and novice basketball players in our psychology lab (Appendix 1), we could write the following:

No difference was observed between the expert and novice players in shooting performance. The performance of both groups was poorer than for those reported by Jones *et al.* (2000) for elite basketball players. The lack of performance differences between novice and expert players is therefore most likely due to the groups being based upon basketball playing experience rather than skill level.

(The reference used above is fictitious.)

Although comparing your data to previous studies is important you must be careful not to be purely descriptive in your approach but to explain any similarities or differences in comparison to your own.

5.4.3 Explain how the results help to answer the research question

When you are planning your discussion it is important to note that what is important or of interest to one author may not be of importance or interest to another. Therefore the focus of a discussion for a given set of results could differ between authors. However, no matter how opinions or approaches may differ between authors your discussion must address your research question. Theoretically this aspect should be straightforward as you have the results of your statistical analysis to inform you whether your results differed between conditions or groups. For example, consider the hypothesis that a group of basketball players who compete regularly would exhibit less anxiety in a high-pressure shoot-out than a novice group of basketball players. If your anxiety data is statistically lower in the trained group you can accept your hypothesis. If there is no difference (or experienced players are more anxious) then you can reject it. Although one result may be more expected than another you can provide a decision on your hypothesis based on the statistical analysis. However, if there are confounding variables that may have affected the data you need to explain them.

5.5 What do your results actually mean?

If you understand how to relate your results to previous literature and how to put your results into context then you are well on the way to understanding what your results actually mean. As well as discussing the main statistical findings it is useful to reflect upon the factors which contributed to your research design and those considered to reduce the potential variability in your data. Furthermore, these factors may also help explain why your results are different from other studies as a result of protocol, population or procedural differences. These factors may therefore help to explain your results, thus putting them in context. The following section will look at general student concerns relating to discussions, biological and statistical significance, and essentially the meaningfulness of your data.

5.5.1 General discussion concerns

Frequently voiced concerns by undergraduate students include 'I haven't found any significance so I have nothing to write about' and 'What happens if my results aren't very good?' Part of this has been answered in Section 5.4.2 with the examples of blood lactate responses to a simulated soccer match and the accuracy of shooting performance in different anxiety conditions. If no differences have been observed between specific comparisons the general responses to a protocol or treatment should be considered (note that these should be considered anyway in terms of the underlying processes). For example:

> No differences were observed between the blood lactate concentrations between midfielders and defenders. However, the values observed for both groups were similar to other simulated soccer protocols (Smith *et al.*, 2003; Jones *et al.*, 2006), demonstrating the imbalance between lactate production and removal during repeated high intensity efforts (Smith and Jones, 2004).

(The references used above are fictitious. Also note that more detail explaining the underlying physiological responses are likely to be expected.)

You should certainly discuss the underlying processes that explain your results for the majority of the variables measured. Discussing responses in this way also helps to put your result into context. Remember that the difference between your study design and previous studies may have been the crux of your research question. Consider the comforting statement from Foote (2009b) that it is not a sign of failure if the results are not as expected.

As regards the student concern that their data is 'not very good' just remember what your project signifies. It is not designed to win Nobel prizes or to produce the basis of a classic research article (although some dissertations may contain publishable data). The aim very often includes demonstrating an ability to undertake an independent piece of research. The data is usually only one part of the assessment. Although you are likely to feel more confident about your discussion if you have clear and good-quality results you still need to discuss them effectively.

With respect to data quality at an undergraduate level you may have some results with large standard deviations or erratic or irregular responses. Here it is best to consider what may be producing these responses. Are the large standard deviations due to outliers? Is there an erroneous value in the spreadsheet that has gone unchecked? Are your resting data responses quite variable but the exercise responses less so? A number of these factors can probably be answered by perusing your data set and explaining the potential reasons in your discussion.

5.5.2 Statistical significance vs. biological significance

If you find that you have no statistically significant data, all is not lost. As well as putting your data into context with previous research you can also put data into context with respect to the biological significance. Biological significance refers to factors such as whether your (non-statistically significant) differences are greater than you may expect with respect to daily variation or measurement error (see Section 3.4). For example, consider a performance trial where there were no statistically significant differences in the mean values but the values appear to be different. You could have a scenario here where all participants improved, but by small amounts, or where no one actually performed worse. You can consider your data on an individual level identifying those participants who performed better than others and those who did not and assess whether these participants exhibited any specific characteristics. Although this approach may be useful for performance data it is by no means a licence to ignore your statistical outputs. If the statistical tests find no difference then there is no difference to report. Many students report in their results section or discussion that 'there were no differences between trials' and then state that one value was greater than another.

Incorporating biological significance may provide greater scope for discussion particularly when you have previously determined the reliability or the magnitude of daily variation for your specific populations and variables of interest. Skelton and Edwards (2000) note that a central aim of the discussion in quantitative research is to reinterpret the significance as relevance and this requires subjective interpretations of the data. The authors further note that future hypotheses are generated from the 'maybe' or 'perhaps' of speculative statements. However, you must be sure not to over-speculate on what your data shows.

Interpreting biological significance is of importance for performance data. Where you are writing athlete feedback reports or case studies it is vital that you know what is a meaningful change or adaptation. As case studies generally have a sample size of one (n = 1) and you are unable to undertake statistical analysis this is particularly important. Some authors have considered that the 'smallest worthwhile change' (Hopkins *et al.*, 1999) in relation to this is worthy of consideration with respect to whether performance may be improved or not.

5.5.3 Effect size and statistical power

Not all undergraduate students will be aware of the concepts of effects size and statistical power. However, these concepts are reasonably straightforward and can help in assessing the meaningfulness of your data. It may seem strange to consider statistical procedures within the discussion rather than in the results, but it is the interpretations of these values which is important, and that occurs within the discussion. As well as the statistical significance you should also consider the practical significance (Vincent, 1999). There a number of measures that can be calculated to help provide additional information to the P value.

Vincent (1999) notes that if the number of participants in an analysis is large, the standard deviations are small and a repeated measure design is used then it is possible to find differences between means that are quite similar. In this situation although you may have a statistical difference how meaningful is it? An estimation of this can be obtained by a number of methods such as omega squared (Thomas and Nelson, 2001) or by calculation of the effect size (Vincent, 1999). The former is an estimate of the total variance which may be explained by the influence of the dependent variable whereas the latter represents the ratio of the mean difference to the standard deviation of the control group or the pooled SD if there is no control group. Effect size values of 0.2 are generally considered to be small, 0.5 moderate and greater than or equal to 0.8 large. These can be used in addition to P values to express the size of the effect achieved.

A large effect size usually results in a greater statistical power. The latter is usually expressed as a percentage of one (i.e. a power value of 0.89 is 89%). With greater statistical power you can be confident in your statistical outputs. Speed and Andersen (2000) provide effect size calculations for a range of commonly used statistical tests. The authors also noted that the reporting of effect size and statistical power was rare within sport and exercise science research and adequate interpretation of them was even rarer. However, considering these values may help guard against Type I and Type II errors and assist in determining the meaningfulness of your data. In addition, Nevill (2000) notes that it is possible to reduce Type I and Type II errors by ensuring that any underlying assumptions of statistical tests are met. Likewise, performing tests for homogeneity of variance and normality of data should always be undertaken prior to your main data analysis.

5.6 Other discussion considerations and common errors

There are a range of common errors which, as for the other sections of your report, can easily be avoided. This section will cover the most common errors, including repeating information from other sections of the report, not discussing the data, presenting key ideas within paragraphs, over-speculation and providing specific information in comparison to previous studies.

5.6.1 Repeating information from other sections of the report

It is important that your discussion does not repeat information or details from other sections of your report (Alexandrov, 2004; Gaafar, 2005; ICMJE, 1997). Common errors in writing discussions include repeating sections of the literature review or introduction, the methods used, or statistical analysis and statistical tests, and restating the results without discussing them. Some of these aspects may have affected your results or the outcomes of your study and therefore require discussion, but discuss them in the context of your research question.

5.6.2 Discussing YOUR data

A common problem for students writing either lab reports or dissertations is not actually discussing their own data. You may have cited previous literature and reported your findings correctly but if you haven't discussed your results it doesn't develop your discussion – the reader will know how your results compared to previous studies but not what is new, novel or important. Another common error is explaining other people's results rather than your own. This is quite an easy trap to fall into – thinking that you have explained why results may differ but with the focus on other people's results rather than your own. You can read other people's results in their articles so make sure that you explain yours.

5.6.3 Presentation of key ideas within each paragraph

Each paragraph should only consider one aspect of interest. If you try and introduce too many arguments or discussion points into one paragraph it can at best result in overly long paragraphs and at worst confuse the reader. Refer to the chapter on introductions (Chapter 2), where it was suggested that you should be able to read each paragraph and provide one or two words to describe what is being discussed. Use that approach for your discussion. You may well have a number of variables that help to explain a response but try not to overwhelm the reader. If you have a range of theories that are pertinent to what you have measured you should use separate paragraphs for each one.

5.6.4 Paragraph structure

Consider the structure of each paragraph that you write. You need to state what you found, how it compares to previous work and what it actually means. Although this does not have to be in any specific order, as your approach may differ depending on each aspect discussed, each sentence should flow easily from one to the next without making the reader ask themselves what the link may be. Consider the model given in Table 5.2. The example below follows this model and demonstrates how the same information may be written in different ways:

> The knee angle at take-off was found to be greater in the experienced long jumpers when compared to the novice jumpers. This was consistent with the work of Smith *et al.* (2010) and demonstrated the differences in jumping technique between groups of athletes that differed in training status.

OR

> Smith *et al.* (2010) observed that more experienced long jumpers exhibited greater knee joint angles at take-off when compared to less experienced athletes. The results of the current study support this finding and emphasise the differences in jumping technique between groups.

(The reference used above is fictitious.)

Table 5.2 Considerations for components of discussion paragraphs

Component	Possible wording
What was the finding?	Variable X was greater in condition 1 when compared to condition 2
How did it compare to previous work?	This is similar to a study by A This is in contrast to a study by B
What does it mean?	The [similar] response demonstrates C and D The [contrasting] response is possibly due to E and F

Although these two examples present the same information in different ways, both are purely descriptive and do not really provide much insight into the underlying reason for the differences in performance. Taking into account the advice from Section 5.4.2, we can add more information to make the paragraph discuss the results in relation to other variables:

> The knee angle at take-off was found to be greater in the experienced long jumpers when compared to the novice jumpers. This is consistent with the work of Smith *et al.* (2010) and demonstrated the differences in jumping technique between groups of athletes that differed in training status. Furthermore, the present study also demonstrated a faster running velocity at take-off in the experienced group and a strong positive correlation between knee angle and jump distance. It is possible that the faster running speeds at take-off could have contributed to differences in knee angle and consequently greater jump distance.

5.6.5 Comparing your results to previous studies

When comparing your data to previous studies don't forget that you can use results from control trials, where no treatment has been administered, for general comparison. This is so even though the studies may have investigated different treatments to your own. For example, consider a study where you have examined the effects of caffeine ingestion on the performance of repeated sprints. You may want to compare your performance data to what is expected for that protocol. However, what do you do if no studies have examined the responses to caffeine ingestion using this protocol (i.e. the reason why you are interested in studying this area) and you are unable to directly compare your data? The simple answer is that you can at least refer to any study's control trial using the same protocol you used for an initial comparison of results. You can then consider the magnitude of any improvements (or decrements) in performance based on previous performance trial data reported in the literature, but for different protocols.

5.6.6 Be specific in your wording

When discussing previous work it is important to make sure you include all the pertinent information regarding the studies that you are citing. The reader is then able to specifically compare the responses reported to those for your results. For example, it is may be useful to clearly state the protocol or exercise intensity used, the specific time of measurement or the questionnaire used. Conversely, don't be too brief and produce writing that can only be understood by experts in the field (Bem, 1995). It is also important to note the direction of any differences noted in previous research. Stating that previous studies observed a difference is not helpful to the reader. Was it an increase or a decrease?

5.6.7 Subheadings

Although some authors suggest that subsections in journal article discussions may break up the flow for the reader (Foote, 2009b) these can have a place in dissertations. Using the same headings as in the results will help to focus your discussion and ensure that you have covered all the variables measured.

5.6.8 Speculation

Although we noted earlier that you are able to speculate what may have happened in your data it is important not to over-speculate, or discuss aspects that are too far-reaching from your data (Skelton, 1994). Try and keep to the facts that you have presented in your results. Skelton (1994) undertook an analysis of original research articles in the *British Journal of General Practice* and noted that markers of uncertainty, i.e. using words like 'may', 'seems' or 'possibly', were common along with speculation. Second, many articles ended with a recommendation that was too imprecise to be operational.

Exercise 5.3: Components of your discussion

Now you have written your discussion try the same exercise as previously suggested for the introduction. Re-read your discussion and write one word alongside each paragraph to describe the key point being discussed and assess the flow of your ideas.

Paragraph 1: ....

Paragraph 2: ....

Paragraph 3: ....

Paragraph 4: ....

Paragraph 5: ....

Paragraph 6: ....

Paragraph 7: ....

Paragraph 8: ....

Paragraph 9: ....

Paragraph 10: ....

Comment of the flow of your discussion:

....

....

....

....

5.7 Conclusions

Your discussion should always end with an appropriate conclusion. This often takes the form 'The results of this study suggest . . .'. However, try and avoid repeating the results without any application or interpretation otherwise you will have merely written a summary of findings rather than a conclusion. It is also helpful to link the conclusions with the goals of the study, but avoid unqualified statements and conclusions not completely supported by the data (ICMJE, 1997).

You may want to consider whether you can relate your data to more than your specific population – can you relate to your findings to field testing as well as lab tests or actual performance? The important thing is to present your take-home message from your study. This should also tie up with the concluding sentence of your abstract.

Exercise 5.4: Planning your conclusions

Now that you have written your discussion, look again at the main findings you have considered and the application of your work. Note these below and develop your conclusions around them. An example is provided after the exercise.

Main finding   **Application**

....

....

....

....

....

....

Conclusions: ....

....

....

....

....

....

....

For example, an important finding would be that experienced basketball players demonstrated a lower decrease in performance under high-anxiety conditions. The application could be to consider how this is achieved in actual basketball games with a concluding sentence relating to the fact that experienced players may exhibit better coping strategies during competitive situations. Further work could then examine this.

5.8 Limitations and future work

5.8.1 Limitations

Your discussion also provides the opportunity to present any limitations that you have identified within your study. As with critical appraisal identifying limitations is not just about finding negative aspects of your work and what might have not gone to plan. Some limitations are readily accepted and you probably could not have done much to prevent them. Don't forget that even the most sophisticated research designs are not perfect.

So, what could be a limitation to your study? Here it is important to consider factors such as your research design and how well it enabled you to answer your research question. There may be factors which, in light of your results and factors that you could not have known before testing or analysing your results, suggest that modifications to your protocols or procedures may be appropriate. This is very common in research. If we had all the answers we wouldn't need to do the research in the first place, so it is common to encounter the need for modifications to protocols, research design or measurements. As a consequence of this your limitations are closely linked to your suggestions for future work. This is particularly important for PhD students where the thesis will contain a number of linked studies that often follow on from each other with respect to research questions and study design.

Typical limitations for undergraduate work include the population tested and how applicable the results are. Your participant population may not have been as well trained as initially thought or you may not get as clear a split between groups in terms of their physiological characteristics as hoped for. There may also be a genuine reason for low participant numbers – for example, the population was not available at that point in the competitive season. However, you would have ideally already considered this in your initial research design and when considering the practicalities of data collection. The exercise protocols used may have been too intense or not intense enough, potentially needing adjustment after pilot testing or your first few trials.

Finally, a note of caution. Two common limitations are often stated by students. The first is having a small number of participants. This may be a limitation to the quality of the data but should really have been addressed in the initial stages of the project through participant recruitment or during data collection if participants dropped out of the study. Working with humans does mean that you have to accommodate such problems, something which all researchers have to contend with. The number of participants is usually the researcher's responsibility and not generally the key limitation of the study. However, if you express your small number of participants in terms of low statistical power and how it may have affected your results this is a much more considered approach to your possible limitation. Second, students may state equipment malfunction or the need to use 'better equipment' as limitations. Your laboratory equipment is likely to be much more up to date and effective than you may think and you should always have a back-up plan for your data collection in case of malfunction or heavy usage by other students. Don't use the limitations to air your personal gripes or views on resources, such comments are likely to just vex your supervisor! There are much more important limitations to consider.

5.8.2 Future work

Standard viva questions for research degree candidates often include 'if you had to do the study again what would you change' or 'what would your next study be?'. As all research is driven by what has gone before your suggestions for future work should be based on what you have found (or not found) and the limitations you have identified. Consider why you undertook your specific study in the first place – most likely as a result of a gap in the literature or a limitation to previous studies. As with your research question, there must be a rationale for future studies you recommend. If they do not relate to your findings or design then you need to be clear as to why they are important. As with reporting limitations, simply stating that future work should use a greater number of participants or more measurements are not well-considered suggestions. Use Exercise 5.5 to try and link your limitations to future work.

Exercise 5.5: Linking your limitations and future work

Use Table 5.3 below to list the factors you think may be considered as limitations to your study and any future research that may overcome them. Two examples are provided to help you.

Table 5.3 Limitations and future work

Potential limitation	Potential future work
Exercise protocol not intense enough	Modification of the existing protocol or development of a new protocol
Participants aerobic fitness too low	Recruit specifically trained athletes or screen participants prior to inclusion in the study
....	....
....	....
....	....
....	....
....	....
....	....
....	....
....	....

5.9 Chapter summary and reflections

In this chapter we have considered how to discuss your results. The organisation of ideas within a discussion, how to put your results into context and what to do if there are no statistically significant differences in your data were also noted. Once your results are discussed you will have unearthed potential limitations to your study which should be related to future work. The discussion should always focus on the research question asked and whether you have been able to answer it. To assess your understanding of discussions answer the following questions:

- What is a discussion?
- How does a discussion differ from an introduction?
- How can you put your results into context?
- How can you discuss your results if there is no significance?
- What should be included in your limitations and future work?
- What are the common errors in discussions?

5.10 Further activities

Go to the website of a journal that you regularly read or are aware of. Find the author guidelines and consider the advice given for writing discussions.

Use the critical appraisal tools to evaluate or critique journal article discussions as you undertake your background reading. You should also try critiquing your own discussion.

Chapter 6

Referencing and general writing tips

In this chapter you will:

6.1 Referencing

Throughout your studies you will be taught how to reference the various sources of information that you use in writing your assignments. You will also no doubt be informed about plagiarism and how referencing all your sources should avoid this problem. Indeed, both referencing and plagiarism are often directly related. Amongst the range of textbooks available to students regarding academic writing many specialise in referencing or at least have chapters dedicated to these areas (for example Deane, 2010; Neville, 2007). In addition, if you were to undertake a literature search for 'plagiarism' you would find many scholarly articles across all research disciplines, such is its importance to academic and other forms of writing. Three potential problems have been associated with referencing, those being the selection of references, the placement of reference citations and the accuracy of references (Foote, 2007). The selection of references was briefly considered in the introduction and discussion chapters. This chapter will provide the basics for referencing and why it is important.

6.1.1 Why reference?

Although the lab report or project you are writing is your own work you will certainly have used various sources to help you develop your research question and explain your findings. Subsequently you will have used other people's work to get to your final conclusions. The information you have used is the evidence on which you have based your reasoning and discussion. One of the key rules of academic writing is to recognise this evidence and attribute it accordingly to those who provided it in the first instance (Creme and Lea, 2006). Therefore, the main aim of referencing is to show the reader where you have borrowed material from (Deane, 2010). However, there is a lot more to referencing than simply avoiding plagiarism (Neville, 2007).

Foote (2007) notes that proper referencing brings authority, credibility and precision to scientific manuscripts. Furthermore, Neville (2007) notes nine reasons why you should reference: tracing the origin of ideas; building a web of ideas; finding your own voice; demonstrating the validity of arguments; spreading knowledge; showing an appreciation of previous work; indicating the influences within your work; avoiding plagiarism; as well as referencing being an essential part of marking criteria. This is why it is important to reference all your sources. There are a number of different referencing systems and you should always follow the guidelines set by your university.

6.1.2 Different types of referencing

The golden rule of referencing is to provide enough information for the reader to be able to quickly find the source you have cited (Neville, 2007). The two main referencing systems used within academic writing are the Harvard and Vancouver systems. Both need to have an in-text citation every time the source is used with a corresponding list of references at the end of the work (Deane, 2010). The most common system in use in sport and exercise science is probably the Harvard system. The American Psychological Association (APA) has a useful online tutorial and explanation of referencing, formatting and writing scientific manuscripts for publication (http://www. apastyle.org). Many journals cite these guidelines as the favoured referencing system. The Harvard system involves 'author–date' referencing. Here the names of the authors for each source and the date of publication (or date of access in the case of websites) are reported within the text. The full details of each source are then provided at the end of the report, usually in alphabetical order. For the Vancouver system, each source is referred to by a number in the text, corresponding to a numbered reference list at the end of the report. In this instance the list is usually in the order in which sources were cited. However, there are variants of both systems in use which can cause confusion amongst students (Deane, 2010). As noted above you should always follow the guidelines set down by your university.

If you refer back to the introduction chapter (Chapter 2) you will have completed Exercise 2.3 ('Extracting and using information'). This exercise involved combining the information you considered important from four abstracts into one sentence or paragraph. When the information was integrated you will have seen that the 'author–date' system was used in different ways. The examples used in Exercise 2.3 involved primary referencing where you have read the original source yourself. If you have not read the original source yourself and quote it from someone else's work then you are using secondary referencing. There is nothing wrong with secondary referencing itself except you are trusting the interpretation of the original data by the authors to be correct (which on the whole it is likely to be). However, if you constantly use secondary referencing your tutors will know that you have not undertaken a particularly detailed literature search yourself and are relying on other people's opinions. There are different ways to cite secondary references in the text and in the reference list and you should consult your specific guidelines. However, always try to read the original document.

6.1.3 Different ways to reference

If you understand the key aspects of referencing and how to integrate them into your report you should be on the way to successful referencing and writing. You will find that within the author guidelines for every journal there will be examples of how to cite the authors and dates effectively. The following examples cover the most common referencing methods you are likely to require. First, three examples of the in-text citation of primary references:

> Price and Campbell (1997) observed that a cadence of 70 rev.min^{-1} elicited greater peak oxygen uptake than 60 rev.min^{-1} during incremental arm crank ergometry.
>
> It was observed that a cadence of 70 rev.min^{-1} elicited greater peak oxygen uptake than 60 rev.min^{-1} during incremental arm crank ergometry (Price and Campbell, 1997).
>
> Studies examining incremental arm crank ergometry protocols have examined crank rate (Price and Campbell, 1997) and ramp rate (Smith *et al.*, 2004).

For secondary references you would normally state 'cited in' within the in-text citation, as follows:

> Price and Campbell (1996; cited in Smith and Price, 2007) observed that a cadence of 70 rev.min^{-1} elicited greater peak oxygen uptake than 60 rev.min^{-1} during incremental arm crank ergometry.

The reference for Smith and Price would be the one contained in the reference list.

If you want to use multiple studies for a given fact this is perfectly acceptable (two or three will usually suffice). You will need to check your university guidelines as to whether they should appear in alphabetical or chronological order. In addition, there are different rules relating to how many authors are cited. In general, one author involves citing the sole author and date. If there are two authors you would state both authors and the date. If there are three or more you generally cite the first author followed by '*et al.*' (meaning 'and others'). However, there are differences between journals and guidelines as to whether you cite all authors in the first instance and then (where there are three or more authors) the first author and *et al.* with every subsequent use.

When citing textbooks you should cite the author and date as for journal articles. When citing textbooks, or specifically chapters in textbooks where the chapter authors are different from the main author or editor of the book, you generally follow the same guidelines as for journal articles. However, in this instance the format of the reference list becomes more involved. The specific chapter is usually referred to first followed by the details of the main book it is contained within. An example is given below. Again, consult your own guidelines for referencing specifics.

Smith, P.M. and Price, M.J. (2007) Upper-body exercise. In E.M. Winter, A.M. Jones, R.C.R. Davidson, P.D. Bromley and T.H. Mercer (eds.), *Sport and Exercise Physiology Testing Guidelines* (138–144). Abingdon: Routledge.

Exercise 6.1: Getting to grips with referencing

Consult your referencing guidelines or those of a recommended journal. For each type of referencing format, using your references, write an example of the in-text citation and how it would appear in the reference list.

Reference/sentence 1 ....

....

....

Format of reference 1 in reference list ....

....

....

Reference/sentence 2 ....

....

....

Format of reference 2 in reference list ....

....

....

Reference/sentence 3 ....

....

....

Format of reference 3 in reference list ....

....

....

6.2 Plagiarism

You must reference all of your sources so that any ideas or statements that are not your own can be attributed to the original authors. If you do not do this you are considered to be trying to pass off other peoples' ideas as your own, which is called plagiarism. Incidences of plagiarism have increased in number considerably in recent years not only due to Internet enabling large amounts of work to be cut and pasted from a whole host of sites but also because of the ready availability of computer packages that can detect plagiarism. Plagiarism is not just a problem for the electronic age, however, and can certainly occur when electronic databases and sources are not used (see McNamee *et al.*, 2007). Plagiarism also includes collusion between students, falsification of data and a range of exam-cheating offences (Neville, 2007). These days all universities and colleges will have some form of plagiarism policy or statement and you should read yours carefully. Many universities also have informative referencing and plagiarism tutorials. The aim of this section is to provide you with some guidance on how to avoid plagiarism based on my experiences of first-year to final-year assignments being processed through plagiarism panels. Three examples of easily avoidable situations are given below.

6.2.1 'Chunking'

Many allegations of plagiarism, certainly at first-year level, may be down to poor referencing, or what is termed 'poor scholarship'. As you progress through your studies, however, this becomes less of an excuse as you are expected to know the specific and appropriate methods for referencing. 'Chunking' refers to large amounts of text being taken from a single source and not written in your own words (i.e. not paraphrased). There may be a cursory reference at the end of the section but this is not enough. You need to write any information you require in your own words. Similarly, if you place a reference after each sentence it will be clear that you have simply cut and pasted a large chunk from one text. If you are able to use your university's plagiarism software prior to submitting your work such an error should be highlighted in the output. Refer to Exercise 2.3 'Extracting and using information' in the chapter on introductions regarding obtaining key information from your sources.

6.2.2 Patch-working

Patch-working refers to where a section of text has been cut and pasted and a number of words from the original text have been replaced by alternative words with the same meaning. Such an error should be evident from any software output. The fact that the section has not been rewritten would be very clear.

6.2.3 Poor note taking

Many students who have had allegations of plagiarism made against them are genuine mistakes and maybe considered as poor scholarship. A common mistake relates to note-taking skills. This is especially true for students who write notes from a given source when researching their project and then days, weeks or even a few hours later use the information in their own written work. The problem arises when the notes taken by the students were not written in their own words as effectively as they may have been (i.e. they were not paraphrased). Consequently, when integrated into the text of their report it is detected by the plagiarism software as identical or exceptionally close to the original. When writing notes from books or journal articles make sure you know what has been written verbatim and what was definitely written in your own words.

6.3 General writing tips

This section is by no means set out to teach students how to write grammatically correct English or even how to write scientifically. There are many excellent texts which already exist relating to those topics. This section is primarily designed to make you aware of what you are writing and how to describe the results of laboratory-based experiments. It is hoped that after reading the examples you will be able to reflect upon and improve your own writing. We are always learning how to write and, although it gets easier with experience, there are always aspects to improve upon. You should also consider the intended audience as the language used will differ. For example, are you writing a report for an athlete, a report to a funding body or an article for a scientific journal? This section will focus upon the conventional scientific report format. However, all types of report require clear concise writing.

There are a considerable number of articles and editorials in scientific journals addressing aspects of journal article production (Greenhalgh, 1997) and key aspects of science such as ethics (Maughan *et al.*, 2007; Winter and Maughan, 2009), peer review (Baltzopoulos, 2004) and scientific writing (Bartlett, 2001; Winter, 2005). With respect to editors' comments on the clarity of manuscripts submitted for publication many authors have their own particular nemeses. However, most editors note that many articles rejected following peer review are often just badly written (Greenhalgh, 1997) and many lack the clarity and precision expected (Baltzopoulos, 2004). Furthermore, the many aspects of journal reviewing considered by reviewers and editors should not just be confined to writing journal articles but also applied to scientific writing in general (Baltzopoulos, 2004). Most journals recommend that manuscripts should be proofread carefully, so why not laboratory reports and theses? Your reports and theses will indeed be read by other people, especially by your assessors. In the case of MSc and PhD theses these will be read by the examiners and possibly by other postgraduate students, and as such reflect you as the author. It is therefore important to make your thesis the best read possible. The aim of this section is to summarise a range of comments from editorials in sport and exercise science journals to emphasise recurrent errors in scientific writing, many of which can be easily avoided. These should be considered in conjunction with classic scientific writing texts such as Day (1998) and Turk and Kirkman (1989), which are often recommended for undergraduate and postgraduate students.

6.3.1 Abbreviations

You will find that many journal articles will abbreviate certain terms to aid the flow of reading. This is particularly evident for labels referring to experimental and control trials. The latter is normally abbreviated to CON and the former to some kind of acronym or shorthand. After this, however, only standard abbreviations should be used and, importantly, written out in full prior to their use. This is a common error of undergraduate students. For example, many students write that '$\dot{V}O_{2max}$ was measured'. If you have not defined this term the reader may not know what $\dot{V}O_{2max}$ refers to, even though you might consider it standard terminology for anyone working in your area. Not everyone reading journal articles in your area will be a student of your discipline. The above example is better written as 'Maximal oxygen uptake ($\dot{V}O_{2max}$) was measured', rather than '$\dot{V}O_{2max}$ (maximal oxygen uptake) was measured'.

Bartlett (2001) notes that abbreviations are essential for mathematical equations but not always within the text of scientific manuscripts. Bartlett further states that although abbreviations may be a 'word-saving device' they can ultimately decrease the readability of the work. Consider the sentence below from a hypothetical study of pre-performance anxiety:

> Pre-performance anxiety (PPA) was measured in elite tennis players (ETP) and club-level players (CLP) during a high-anxiety (HA) condition and a control condition (CON). Heart rate (HR) was also measured to determine the severity of somatic anxiety (SOM).

If all terms had been abbreviated and used throughout the manuscript the sentence may read as follows:

> PPA was measured in ETP and CLP during an HA trial and CON. HR was also measured to determine the severity of SOM.

Although the word count is considerably reduced in the second passage the reader has to remember a large number of definitions, many of which are not standard or regularly used. This is one reason why nonstandard abbreviations are avoided. If you are using abbreviations, avoid starting sentences with the abbreviated form and avoid back-to-back abbreviations.

6.3.2 Readability

An important attribute of any piece of written work is its readability (Bartlett, 2001). Indeed, the readability of any manuscript is considered to be critical for communication and understanding (Winter, 2005). Within word processing documents you are able to assess the readability of your work. For example, Microsoft Word allows you to assess the readability of your work using the Flesch Reading Ease test and the Flesch-Kincaid Grade Level test. Both tests assess the readability of your work based on the length of sentences and the number of syllables per sentence. The former test provides a score out of 100 whereas the latter provides a grading based on the American school system of grades. The example provided by the Word Help menu states that if you have a grade score of 8.0 a student in the eighth grade should be able to read it successfully. Try activating the analysis as directed by the Help menu to determine your own readability scores. It may be quite enlightening!

6.3.3 Grammar and paragraph structure

In a large number of reports, and not just from first-year students, there is often a lack of proper sentence construction and paragraph structure. Each sentence should ideally provide one main fact or idea. Sentences should be concise, not overly long and punctuated appropriately. If you have a sentence that is more than two or three lines long it is probably too long. Sentences are then linked together to form paragraphs. I am often amazed at the number of reports where sentences are presented separately, appearing on a new line rather than in paragraph form. Paragraphs should link sentences together to provide one key and coherent idea for the reader. Throughout this book it has been suggested that you read each paragraph of your work and use one word to see what the content reflects. You could also try reading the first and last lines of each paragraph to see whether the main idea is clearly introduced and concluded.

6.3.4 Writing style and word use

Every author will develop their own writing style with time and experience and it is not the purpose of texts such as this to enforce a standardised writing style upon students. However, there are a number of factors emphasised by journal editors that should be considered by those writing regularly. If you consider the comments below and put them into practice your understanding of phrasing and wording should hopefully be much improved and the clarity of your writing style enhanced.

Bartlett (2001) considered the excessive use of the 'passive voice' in writing and how it may hinder readability. Three specific examples were provided: using more words than is necessary; using meaningless or filler words; and the correct use of words. When considering the use of more words than necessary, students are often concerned with word counts, so any word-saving approach should be well received. The examples given included stating 'the majority of' compared to simply saying 'most' and stating 'due to the fact that' instead of 'because'. Examples such as these may help to reduce the sometimes 'flowery' nature of some writing in an attempt to impress the tutor or make the writing appear more important. Using extra words can overcomplicate what you are saying, when essentially you just need to get to the point.

Examples of the use of meaningless and filler words included stating 'game situation' instead of 'game' or 'measures of anxiety levels' instead of 'measures of anxiety'. In relation to this latter example and the correct use of words, Bartlett (2001) notes that the correct use of the word 'level' is in 'level playing field', 'sea level' and 'liquid level'. Therefore, when describing the performance ability of participants 'national level' should be replaced by 'national standard'. Similarly, 'force levels' should be referred to as the 'magnitude of force'. An example from my own experience relates to using 'lactate levels' where 'blood lactate concentration' should be correctly used instead. Similarly, the word 'higher' is often misused. If a participant's heart rate has increased it should be described using 'greater' rather than 'higher', as higher pertains to height. This can also be applied to blood lactate concentration and other sport and exercise related variables that may change with exercise.

Four further examples of common writing errors termed as 'brow furrowing writing' were provided by Winter (2005). The first example was the use of vernacular, such as stating 'This study looked at' rather than studies 'investigating' or 'examining'. The second example was tautology, such as stating 'There are many different types'. Winter notes that if there are many types then they must be different so the word different is not required. The third example, superfluousness, relates to Bartlett's comment about extra words being used, such as 'in order'. Omitting these words makes no difference to the sentence so they can be removed. Finally, the phrase 'Participants were familiarised with procedures' was considered. Winter suggests it is better to phrase participants being familiarised as being 'habituated', 'accustomed' or 'well-practised'.

6.3.5 Punctuation

Most word processing software packages have both spelling and grammar checkers that can monitor your punctuation and sentence structure, usually providing indications of errors as you write. Even if you do not understand the grammatical terminology used to explain the errors, grammar checkers generally provide alternative ways of constructing your sentences which may help develop your writing. However, you should always try and develop your own writing style. A simple and common mistake is the misuse and overuse of commas. Commas can be used in a number of ways such as for lists and to add extra information or context within a sentence. For example, consider the following sentence:

> The exercise protocol, which was undertaken by ten male participants, involved incremental exercise to exhaustion.

If the text between the commas is removed the general message of the sentence should not be affected. In other words:

> The exercise protocol involved incremental exercise to exhaustion.

Commas are often overused and can hinder the readability of your sentences. If you are using a large number of commas and your sentences are long consider splitting the sentence up into separate, more concise ones.

6.4 Common errors

There is a range of writing errors commonly noted by tutors when assessing work. Many can be avoided by careful proofreading. The following are some examples to watch out for.

6.4.1 Incorrect word use

Although we have considered using the correct words in describing how variables may differ between treatments (e.g. 'higher' vs. 'greater') there is a much simpler error and one that is not detected by spell checkers. In this instance the word is spelt correctly but is just the wrong word. Common examples are shown in Table 6.1. My particular favourites over the years have been the 'lactate shuffle' and 'hydrogen iron'.

6.4.2 In-text citation errors

We have briefly considered the citation of previous studies within your work using the author–date system. A key error is stating the author's initials, journal title or any other information in the text that should only be contained within the reference list. This shows your assessor that you have not grasped the format of referencing within the text. Only the name and date is required in the text.

6.4.3 Omission of cited references

If you cite a source of information it must be contained within the reference list (exceptions to this rule are 'personal communications' or articles 'in press', although these forms of referencing are unlikely to affect you during your undergraduate studies). A common error is to cite a study and not provide the details within the reference list or, conversely, listing a reference that has not been cited in the text. All the sources in the reference list must be used in the text and vice versa. A list of all the sources you have used in preparation for the report (i.e. background reading, etc. and those sources not necessarily used for writing the report) is termed a 'bibliography'. However, we do not use bibliographies for academic writing.

6.4.4 Not reading original sources

Wherever possible it is recommended that you obtain and read the original journal article or source of information. It is unlikely that many students will obtain original articles with publication dates prior to 1970, as this is the date where some search

Table 6.1 Common wording errors

Affect/effect
There/their/they're
Ion/Iron
Sources/sauces
To/too/two
Previous/pervious

engines may not have abstracts available or online access. However, reading much older articles is very useful for becoming aware of how research has developed over time. If you cite much older articles your tutors will probably, and often correctly, presume that you have not read the original article, even though you may have correctly listed the source in your reference list. A similar problem occurs if you do use an older research article or review article and take a lot of secondary references from it without acknowledging them properly. Here, you will have a lot of older references in your work and the field of research may have moved on considerably in the last 30 or 40 years. This demonstrates to your assessors that you have not fully reviewed the literature and are overreliant on a potentially outdated source. Some students however, may very much enjoy scouring original articles from the early twentieth century – and I do recommend it!

6.4.5 Use of quotes

To avoid disjointed writing and the potential for plagiarism to occur you should avoid using quotes. As you will have seen from your background reading it is very unusual for direct quotes to be used within sport and exercise science. The best method is to paraphrase the information you are interested in and identify the key results in your own words.

6.4.6 Singular vs. plural

A basic grammatical error concerns the use of singular or plural forms of words and descriptions. These are often highlighted on your word processing document as you write and should be taken note of. These errors are generally quite straightforward to correct. For example, the plural of 'was' is 'were', so stating 'Ground reaction forces and running time *was* measured' should be 'Ground reaction forces and running time *were* measured'. The second version is correct as there are two factors being considered, not one, so it is plural. Another example is the use of the word data, which is the plural of datum. This is often confused by students, such as 'data was analysed' rather than 'data were analysed'.

6.5 Formatting a thesis

When you are putting your lab report together you will normally only need the headings of abstract, introduction, methods, results and discussion. However, for a thesis you are likely to have chapter and section numbers to organise. There will no doubt be specific university guidelines for the format and structure of your undergraduate and postgraduate theses but if not, the following may help when organising your headings. The organisation itself is relatively straightforward. The difficulty may arise in ensuring that the content of your section relates to the specific subheadings used. The example shown in Figure 6.1 is typical and there are not usually more divisions of subsections past the third level (the use of i, ii, iii, iv, etc.). Remember, you do not have to separate each section with a different heading if it is not required. As a further example, this text has been organised using typical chapter and section numbering throughout.

```
1.0   Main chapter title (e.g. Introduction/literature review, etc.)
   1.1   Subheading level 1 (e.g. Anxiety and performance)
      1.1.1   Subheading 2 (e.g. Anxiety and team sports)
         1.1.1.i   Subheading level 3 (e.g. Netball)
         1.1.1.ii  Subheading level 3 (e.g. Hockey)
      1.1.2   Subheading level 2 (e.g. Anxiety and individual sports)
         1.1.2.i   Subheading level 3 (e.g. Tennis)
         1.1.2.ii  Subheading level 3 (e.g. Athletics)
   1.2   Measurement of anxiety
      1.2.1   Physiological measures
      1.2.2   Questionnaire methods
      Etc.
```

Figure 6.1 Typical organisation of chapter headings and subheadings

6.6 Appendices

Within your project you may want to present some detailed information which may distract from the key point of the section and affect the flow of writing. Here you may find presenting information in appendices is more appropriate. Appendices are usually used for more methodological aspects such as presenting perceptual scales or full versions of questionaires that have been used. The reader can then refer to the appendix if they are unfamiliar with the item or if they require further more specific information. Long descriptions of biochemical methods or calibration procedures can also be presented here, in the absence of a general methods section.

6.7 A final note

Always proofread your work before you submit it as this will avoid many errors. Take time to do this rather than rushing it as you may miss more subtle, but important, errors. You may be able to see your tutors regarding coursework on a number of occasions prior to submission of your work. If you take advantage of this chance make sure you turn up prepared with ideas and ideally a draft of your work. Also, do this early as there will probably be a long queue of fellow students outside your tutor's door the week before the submission date!

Once you have received the mark for your work always read the feedback provided by your tutors. If you cannot read their handwriting go and see them for clarification or further feedback. Remember to read any generic feedback documents that are provided. This will help you reflect upon your work and should help you improve for the next assignment. Finally, make sure you have a back-up of your work in case of loss of files or damage to your data storage device.

6.8 Chapter summary and reflections

In this chapter we have considered why referencing is important and how to reference your information sources. We have also considered plagiarism and a range of techniques to avoid it. The second section of this chapter covered some general writing tips as noted by journal editors and how these may affect the flow of your writing. Finally, we considered the organisation of your thesis with respect to numbering chapters and headings. To assess your understanding of this chapter answer the following questions:

- Why is referencing important?
- What types of referencing systems are there?
- What is plagiarism?
- What are the common referencing and writing errors?

6.9 Further activities

Go to the website of a journal that you regularly read or are aware of. Find the author guidelines and consider the advice given for referencing. Also refer to the journal articles that you read to see how the types of referencing and use of citations may differ.

Activate the readability function within the spelling and grammar checkers of your word processing software and assess the first and final drafts of your work.

Appendix 1: Example data and experimental details for typical sport and exercise science labs and projects

A: Lab report 1 – Maximal oxygen uptake

Study

$\dot{V}O_{2max}$ assessed in a group of fit healthy sport science students treadmill running, cycling and arm ergometry.

Participants

N = 10 healthy university students, all recreationally active but none specifically trained.

Age (years)	19.3 (2.6)
Height (m)	1.79 (0.08)
Body mass (kg)	71.2 (7.1)

Protocols

Table A.1 Exercise protocols undertaken to determine maximal oxygen uptake ($\dot{V}O_{2max}$) for treadmill running, cycle ergometry and arm cranking

	Treadmill	Cycle ergometry	Arm cranking
Initial intensity	8 km.h^{-1}	70 W	50 W
Cadence	–	70 rev.min^{-1}	70 rev.min^{-1}
Exercise stage duration	3 min	3 min	2 min
Exercise intensity Increment	2 km.h^{-1}	35 W	20 W

Oxygen consumption determined from Douglas bag technique in the final minute of exercise.

Heart rate continually monitored using a heart rate monitor.

Exercise testing performed at the same time of day. At least 5 days between tests.

Data

Data provided for maximal/peak oxygen uptake ($\dot{V}O_{2max}/\dot{V}O_{2peak}$; ml.kg^{-1}min^{-1}) and maximal/peak heart rate (HR$_{max}$/HR$_{peak}$; beats.min^{-1}).

	$\dot{V}O_{2max}/\dot{V}O_{2peak}$			HR_{max}/HR_{peak}		
	Treadmill	Cycling	Arm crank	Treadmill	Cycling	Arm crank
1	61.0	55.4	43.8	191	187	181
2	59.6	53.7	41.9	187	181	175
3	45.3	40.7	31.6	193	185	181
4	51.5	49.1	29.5	196	190	183
5	56.8	53.1	45.6	201	195	187
6	63.1	57.7	36.1	198	191	171
7	66.3	60.5	49.7	189	179	169
8	58.9	53.6	37.4	195	181	178
9	59.6	52.4	36.1	187	183	180
10	62.9	57.2	35.3	199	191	189
Mean	58.5	53.3	38.7	194	186	179
SD	6.1	5.5	6.4	5	5	6

Results

Maximal/peak oxygen consumption
Analysed by one-way ANOVA.
Significant difference ($P < 0.05$) between exercise modes.
Treadmill and cycle ergometry $\dot{V}O_{2max}$ were greater than for arm cranking.
Treadmill was greater than cycle ergometry.

Maximal/peak heart rate
Analysed by one-way ANOVA.
Significant difference ($P < 0.05$) between exercise modes.
Treadmill and cycle ergometry $\dot{V}O_{2max}$ were greater than for arm cranking.
Treadmill was greater than cycle ergometry.

B: Lab report 2 – Anxiety laboratory

Study
The effects of low and high anxiety levels on basketball shooting performance in a group of novice and experienced university basketball players.

Participants
N = 10 in each group; novice players had been competing for less than two years, expert players had been competing for more than five years.

	Novice	Expert
Age (years)	18.9 (1.9)	19.1 (2.3)
Height (m)	1.87 (0.15)	1.81 (0.13)
Body mass (kg)	81.2 (6.1)	83.6 (5.4)
Experience (years)	1.7 (0.6)	8.3 (0.8)

Protocols

Participants took 15 basketball shots under both low- and high-anxiety conditions. The low-anxiety condition was undertaken on a basketball court with only the experimenter present. The high-anxiety condition was undertaken on the same basketball court with the full basketball squad present (n = 30 players) producing a noisy atmosphere similar to competition. The number of baskets scored was the performance measure.

Heart rate was measured using a heart rate monitor to give an indication of the level of anxiety.

Data

Data provided for average heart rate during each trial (HR; beats.min^{-1}) and baskets scored (n/15 shots).

		Heart rate		Baskets scored	
		Low anxiety	High anxiety	Low anxiety	High anxiety
Novice	1	123	141	10	5
	2	128	135	11	7
	3	111	128	12	8
	4	118	131	13	7
	5	120	137	9	7
	6	118	143	11	8
	7	109	134	12	7
	8	127	142	7	6
	9	116	131	8	3
	10	109	126	9	7
Mean		118	135	10	7
SD		7	6	2	2
Expert	1	118	125	14	13
	2	116	131	13	13
	3	115	120	12	10
	4	120	129	11	11
	5	115	120	13	12
	6	107	119	12	10
	7	101	123	13	12
	8	119	124	13	11
	9	108	117	11	11
	10	101	121	10	9
Mean		112	123	12	11
SD		7	4	1	1

Results

Mean heart rate

Analysed by two-way ANOVA.

Significant main effects ($P < 0.05$) for conditions (anxiety level) and experiences (novice vs. expert).

Baskets scored

Analysed by two-way ANOVA.

Significant interaction ($P < 0.05$) between conditions.

Post hoc analysis indicated that performance was poorer for the novice players in the high-anxiety condition ($P < 0.05$) when compared to low-anxiety conditions.

Performance was lower in both low- and high-anxiety conditions in the novice players when compared to the expert players.

C: Lab report 3 – Ground reaction forces

Study

Ground reaction forces measured during walking and running at two different speeds.

Participants

N = 8 healthy university students, all recreationally active but none specifically trained.

Age (years)	20.1 (2.4)
Height (m)	1.75 (0.07)
Body mass (kg)	68.2 (8.1)

Protocols

Ground reaction forces assessed using a force plate. Each participant had three attempts at each speed to provide as constant a speed as possible. Walking and running speed was monitored using timing gates. Participants were asked to walk at their usual walking speed and run at a jog and moderate speeds. Speeds were approximately 1.0, 2.5 and 4.0 m.sec^{-1}.

All trials were performed on the same time of day and on the same day.

Data

Data provided for ground reaction force ($\times$ body mass) and walking/running speed (m.sec^{-1}).

		Ground reaction forces			Speeds		
		Walk	*Jog*	*Run*	*Walk*	*Jog*	*Run*
	1	0.90	1.45	3.25	1.04	2.51	4.13
	2	0.95	1.53	3.35	1.23	2.48	4.56
	3	1.01	1.67	2.89	1.15	2.35	3.99
	4	1.05	1.64	3.25	1.21	2.67	3.87
	5	0.99	1.57	3.45	1.05	2.78	3.76
	6	0.87	1.49	3.15	0.95	2.12	4.42
	7	1.04	1.51	2.91	0.97	2.55	4.38
	8	1.10	1.67	3.08	0.89	2.76	3.81
Mean		0.99	1.57	3.17	1.06	2.53	4.12
SD		0.08	0.09	0.20	0.12	0.22	0.31

Results

Peak ground reaction force (× body mass)
Analysed by one-way ANOVA.
Significant difference ($P < 0.05$) between walking/running speeds.
All trials significantly different from each other.

Walking/running speed
Analysed by one-way ANOVA.
Significant difference ($P < 0.05$) between walking/running speeds.
All trials significantly different from each other.

Appendix 2: Procedure for formatting V̇ in Microsoft Word

1. From the Insert menu click on Object (or hold down ALT and I together and then O on its own).
2. Scroll down the options and double-click Microsoft equation 3.0. The Equation tool bar will be shown. If you hover your mouse arrow over the bar's options you will see the following: relational symbols, spaces and ellipses, embellishments, etc.
3. Type 'V' (or whatever letter is required) to the text box provided.
4. Then click on Embellishments and choose the option required (i.e. a dot over the centre of the character [represented by the grey box], third line down). The line spacing will be disrupted a little but this can be overcome by using the line spacing option in the format paragraph options.

Appendix 3: Answers to Chapter 4 exercises

A: Typical figures for a range of experimental designs for Exercise 4.1

Data set	Potential figure
Relationship between personality score and performance anxiety	Scatter plot
Differences between centre of gravity at heel strike during running in elite and novice runners	Block graph
Difference in peak power during a Wingate Anaerobic test in a group of cyclists before and after 8 weeks of sprint training	Block graph
Maximal oxygen uptake in a group of runners during two different exercise protocols	Block graph for means Scatter plot for relationship between them
Motivation to train in international male rowers, national-level female rowers and club-level rowers	Block graph
Blood pH at rest and during interval training	Time-based figure (line or scatter plot with straight lines between)
Core temperature at rest and during prolonged exercise on two occasions, one where participants could drink and one where they could not	Time-based figure (line or scatter plot with straight lines between)

B: Experimental designs to be analysed statistically for Exercise 4.4

Data set	*Potential test*
Relationship between personality score and performance anxiety	Correlation
Differences between centre of gravity at heel strike during running in elite and novice runners	Independent t-test
Difference in peak power during a Wingate Anaerobic test in a group of cyclists before and after 8 weeks of sprint training	Dependent/paired t-test
Maximal oxygen uptake in a group of runners during two different exercise protocols	Both t-test and correlation
Motivation to train in international rowers, national-level rowers and club-level rowers	One-way ANOVA
Blood pH at rest and during interval training	One-way ANOVA with repeated measure
Core temperature at rest and during prolonged exercise on two occasions, one where participants could drink and one where they could not	Two-way ANOVA with repeated measures

C: Written examples for Exercises 4.6, 4.7, 4.9, 4.10 and 4.12

Answers for Exercise 4.6

You could describe this result in any of the following ways:

1. The correlation between anxiety and introversion was significant ($r = 0.973$, $P < 0.05$).
2. The correlation between anxiety and introversion ($r = 0.973$) was significant ($P < 0.05$).
3. The relationship between anxiety and introversion provided a correlation of $r = 0.973$ ($P < 0.05$).

If you have multiple variables, such as in Table 4.9, you could word your description as follows:

A summary of correlations between key variables is shown in Table 4.9. Strong positive correlations were observed for RPE against heart rate ($r = 0.972$), blood lactate ($r = 0.958$) and oxygen consumption ($r = 0.947$; $P < 0.05$). A moderate negative correlation was observed for pH and blood lactate ($r = 0.770$; $P < 0.05$).

If you have a large number of correlations you can provide a table based on the r values from the correlation matrix. However, make sure that only the meaningful values are presented.

Answers for Exercise 4.7

The t-test results in Table 4.10 could be reported as follows:

> The motivation to train in elite athletes was greater than for non-elite athletes ($P < 0.05$).

Adding some descriptive values would result in the following:

> The motivation to train in elite athletes (20.2 ± 2.4) was greater than for non-elite athletes 12.1 (± 3.6) ($P < 0.05$).

Alternatively, you could write:

> The motivation to train in elite athletes was 20.2 ± 2.4, whereas for the non-elite athletes it was 12.1 ± 3.6. The difference between groups was significant ($t_{(18)} = 5.95$; $P < 0.05$).

Answers for Exercise 4.9

From the statistical outputs above you could report the results in the following ways:

1. There was a significant difference between groups for long jump distance ($P < 0.05$) with the senior athletes achieving greater distances (7.73 ± 0.18 m) than both the under-19 athletes (7.30 ± 0.18 m; $P < 0.05$) and the under-21 athletes (7.47 ± 0.17 m).

2. There was a significant difference between groups for long jump distance ($F_{(2,21)} = 11.642$; $P < 0.05$) with the senior athletes achieving greater distances (7.73 ± 0.18 m) than both the under-19 athletes (7.30 ± 0.18 m; $P < 0.05$) and the under-21 athletes (7.47 ± 0.17 m).

3. There was a significant difference in long jump performance between groups ($P < 0.05$). Post hoc analysis revealed differences between the under-19 and senior athletes and the under-21 and senior athletes but no differences between the under-21 athletes and under-19 athletes.

4. Long jump distances for the U19, U21 and senior athletes were 7.30 ± 0.18, 7.47 ± 0.17 and 7.73 ± 0.18 m, respectively ($P < 0.05$). Distances for the U19 and senior athletes and the U21 and senior groups were significantly different ($P < 0.05$), whereas those for the U19 and U21 athletes were not ($P > 0.05$).

5. Long jump distances for the U19, U21 and senior athletes were 7.30 ± 0.18, 7.47 ± 0.17 and 7.73 ± 0.18 m, respectively ($F_{(2,21)} = 11.642$; $P < 0.05$). Distances for the U19 and senior athletes and the U21 and senior groups were significantly different ($P < 0.05$), whereas those for the U19 and U21 athletes were not ($P > 0.05$).

Notice that the term 'respectively' is used within the written description above. This is commonly used in journal articles and scientific analyses to enable a list of values to be given in relation to the trials they belong to without requiring too much repetition in the text. Also note that use of '$P > 0.05$' when significant is *not* found.

Answer for Exercise 4.10

You could report this data in the following way:

Blood lactate concentration at rest and during exercise for the two training types is shown in Figure 4.11. A significant interaction was observed ($P < 0.05$). There were no differences for resting values between trials (1.3 ± 0.4 and 1.2 ± 0.3 mmol.l^{-1} for CON and INT, respectively; $P > 0.05$) with blood lactate concentration increasing from rest at 4 minutes in both trials (4.8 ± 0.6 and 5.4 ± 0.6 mmol.l^{-1}, respectively; $P > 0.05$). During interval training blood lactate continued to increase from this point until the end of exercise (7.5 ± 0.6 mmol.l^{-1}; $P < 0.05$) whereas values decreased during the continuous trial (3.3 ± 0.7 mmol.l^{-1}; $P < 0.05$). Blood lactate at the end of exercise was greater following INT than for CON ($P < 0.05$).

Answer for Exercise 4.12

Comments for written description 1 could include:

1. Specific figure is not stated.
2. Specific trial where greater values are found is not stated.
3. No description of values obtained.
4. Where were the differences found between trials?

Comments for written description 2 could include:

1. Specific figure is not stated.
2. Every mean is provided in the description making it more of a catalogues of values than a true description of key results.
3. No standard deviations are provided.
4. No statistical results are provided.

You could report this data in the following way:

Ratings of perceived exertion (RPE) for both the fast and slow music trials are shown in Figure 4.12. There was no interaction observed between music tempo and time ($F_{(3,48)} = 0.32$; $P > 0.05$). However, significant main effects were observed for music tempo ($F_{(1,48)} = 31.17$; $P < 0.05$) and time ($F_{(3,48)} = 8.52$; $P < 0.05$). RPE for the fast tempo trial was consistently greater than for the slow tempo trial ($P < 0.05$). RPE increased from values at 5 minutes of exercise (12.3 ± 1.1 and 13.4 ± 0.8 for the slow and fast tempos, respectively) to 13.4 ± 0.8 and 14.9 ± 0.9 at 15 minutes. Values then remained at similar levels until the end of exercise (13.9 ± 1.1 and 15.0 ± 0.8, respectively).

Appendix 4: Statistical outputs for Excel

A: Lab report 1 – Maximal oxygen uptake

Maximal/peak oxygen consumption
ANOVA: single factor

SUMMARY

Groups	Count	Sum	Average	Variance
Treadmill	10	585	58.5	37.36889
Cycling	10	533.4	53.34	29.81156
Arm cranking	10	387	38.7	40.74222

ANOVA

Source of variation	SS	df	MS	F	P-value	F crit
Between groups	2109.984	2	1054.992	29.32633	1.7E-07	3.354131
Within groups	971.304	27	35.97422			
Total	3081.288	29				

Maximal/peak heart rate
ANOVA: single factor

SUMMARY

Groups	Count	Sum	Average	Variance
Treadmill	10	1936	193.6	25.15556
Cycling	10	1863	186.3	28.45556
Arm cranking	10	1794	179.4	40.93333

ANOVA

Source of variation	SS	df	MS	F	P-value	F crit
Between groups	1008.467	2	504.2333	15.99988	2.61E-05	3.354131
Within groups	850.9	27	31.51481			
Total	1859.367	29				

B: Lab report 2 – Anxiety lab class

Mean heart rate in low- and high-anxiety conditions
ANOVA: two-factor with replication

SUMMARY

	Low anxiety	High anxiety	Total
Novice			
Count	10	10	20
Sum	1179	1348	2527
Average	117.9	134.8	126.35
Variance	47.21111111	35.06666667	114.1342
Expert			
Count	10	10	20
Sum	1120	1229	2349
Average	112	122.9	117.45
Variance	51.77777778	19.87777778	65.20789
Total			
Count	20	20	
Sum	2299	2577	
Average	114.95	128.85	
Variance	56.05	63.29210526	

ANOVA

Source of variation	SS	df	MS	F	P-value
Sample	792.1	1	792.1	20.58294	6.13E-05
Columns	1932.1	1	1932.1	50.20615	2.54E-08
Interaction	90	1	90	2.338675	0.134937
Within	1385.4	36	38.48333		
Total	4199.6	39			

Baskets scored in low- and high-anxiety conditions
ANOVA: two-factor with replication

SUMMARY

	Low anxiety	High anxiety	Total
Novice			
Count	10	10	20
Sum	102	65	167
Average	10.2	6.5	8.35
Variance	3.733333333	2.277777778	6.45
Expert			
Count	10	10	20
Sum	122	112	234
Average	12.2	11.2	11.7
Variance	1.511111111	1.733333333	1.8
Total			
Count	20	20	
Sum	224	177	
Average	11.2	8.85	
Variance	3.536842105	7.713157895	

ANOVA

Source of variation	SS	df	MS	F	P-value	F crit
Sample	112.225	1	112.225	48.5006	3.66E-08	4.113165
Columns	55.225	1	55.225	23.86675	2.13E-05	4.113165
Interaction	18.225	1	18.225	7.876351	0.008032	4.113165
Within	83.3	36	2.313889			
Total	268.975	39				

C: Lab report 3 – Ground reaction forces

Ground reaction forces
ANOVA: single factor

SUMMARY

Groups	Count	Sum	Average	Variance
Walk	8	7.92	0.99	0.005857
Jog	8	12.53	1.56625	0.007255
Run	8	25.33	3.16625	0.039713

ANOVA

Source of variation	SS	df	MS	F	P-value	F crit
Between groups	20.34168	2	10.17084	577.615	4.4E-19	3.4668
Within groups	0.369775	21	0.017608			
Total	20.71145	23				

Walking/running speeds
ANOVA: single factor

SUMMARY

Groups	Count	Sum	Average	Variance
Walk	8	8.49	1.06125	0.015584
Jog	8	20.22	2.5275	0.048393
Run	8	32.92	4.115	0.093743

ANOVA

Source of variation	SS	df	MS	F	P-value	F crit
Between groups	37.32116	2	18.66058	354.9446	6.5E-17	3.4668
Within groups	1.104038	21	0.052573			
Total	38.4252	23				

References

Alexandrov, A.V. (2004) How to write a research paper. *Cerebrovasc Dis* **18**, 135–8.

Alexandrov, A.V. and Hennerici, M.G. (2007) Writing good abstracts. *Cerebrovasc Dis* **23**(4), 256–9.

Altinörs, N. (2002) The structure of a neurosurgical manuscript. *Acta Neurochir Suppl* **83**, 115–20.

Andreacci, J.L., LeMura, L.M., Cohen, S.L., Urbansky, E.A., Chelland, S.A. and Von Duvillard, S.P. (2002) The effects of frequency of encouragement on performance during maximal exercise testing. *J Sports Sci* **20**(4), 345–52.

Annesley, T.M. (2010) Bring your best to the table. *Clin Chem* **56**(10), 1528–34.

Artioli, G.G., Gualano, B., Coelho, D.F., Benatti, F.B., Gailey, A.W. and Lancha, A.H. Jr. (2007) Does sodium-bicarbonate ingestion improve simulated judo performance? *Int J Sport Nutr Exerc Metab* **17**(2), 206–17.

Astorino, T.A., Tam, P.A., Rietschel, J.C., Johnson, S.M. and Freedman, T.P. (2004) Changes in physical fitness parameters during a competitive field hockey season. *J Strength Cond Res* **18**(4), 850–4.

Atkinson, G. and Reilly, T. (1996) Circadian variation in sports performance. *Sports Med* **21**(4), 292–312.

Azevedo, L.F., Canário-Almeida, F., Almeida Fonseca, J., Costa-Pereira, A., Winck, J.C. and Hespanhol, V. (2011) How to write a scientific paper: writing the methods section. *Rev Port Pneumol* **17**(5), 232–8.

Baltzopoulos, V. (2004) The reviewing process. *J Sports Sci*, **22**(2), 147–8.

Bartlett, R. (2001) Writing for the Journal of Sports Sciences. *J Sports Sci*, **19**(7), 467–8.

Bem, D. (1995) Writing a review article for Psychological Bulletin. *Psychol Bull* **118**(2), 172–7.

Bland, J.M. and Altman, D.G. (1986) Statistical methods for assessing agreement between two methods of clinical measurement. *Lancet* **81**(8476), 307–10.

Bland, J.M. and Altman, D.G. (1995) Comparing two methods of clinical measurement: a personal history. *Int J Epidemiol* **24**(Suppl 1), S7–14.

Bleakley, C. and MacAuley, D. (2002) The quality of research in sports journals. *Br J Sports Med* **36**(2), 124–5.

Borg, G.A. (1973) Perceived exertion: a note on 'history' and methods. *Med Sci Sports* **5**, 90–3.

Bougault, V., Lonsdorfer-Wolf, E., Charloux, A., Richard, R., Geny, B. and Oswald-Mammosser, M. (2005) Does thoracic bioimpedance accurately determine cardiac output in COPD patients during maximal or intermittent exercise? *Chest* **127**(4), 1122–31.

Branson, R.D. (2004) Anatomy of a research paper. *Respir Care* **49**(10), 1222–8.

Brink, Y. and Louw, Q.A. (2011) Clinical instruments: reliability and validity critical appraisal. *J Eval Clin Pract* Jun 20. doi: 10.1111/j.1365-2753.2011.01707.x.

British Medical Journal (1996) Declaration of Helsinki (1964). *BMJ* **313**. doi: 10.1136/bmj.313.7070.1448a.

Brozek, J., Grande, F., Anderson, J.T. and Keys, A. (1963) Densitometric analysis of body composition: revision of some quantitative assumptions. *Ann NY Acad Sci* **110**, 113–40.

Burrows, M. and Bird, S. (2000) The physiology of the highly trained female endurance runner. *Sports Med* **30**(4), 281–300.

Burrows, M. (2007) Circadian rhythms. In E.M. Winter, A.M. Jones, R.C.R. Davidson, P.D. Bromley and T.H. Mercer (eds) *Sport and Exercise Physiology Testing Guidelines*, 347–57. Abingdon: Routledge.

Campbell, S.C., Moffatt, R.J. and Kushnick, M.R. (2011) Continuous and intermittent walking alters HDL(2)-C and LCATa. *Atherosclerosis* **218**(2), 524–9.

Charkoudian, N. and Joyner, M.J. (2004) Physiologic considerations for exercise performance in women. *Clin Chest Med* **25**(2), 247–55.

Christmass, M.A., Dawson, B., Passeretto, P. and Arthur, P.G. (1999) A comparison of skeletal muscle oxygenation and fuel use in sustained continuous and intermittent exercise. *Eur J Appl Physiol Occup Physiol* **80**(5), 423–35.

Clarke, M. and Chalmers, I. (1998) Discussion sections in reports of controlled trials published in general medical journals islands in search of continents? *JAMA* **280**, 280–2.

Clarke, M., Alderson, P. and Chalmers, I. (2002) Discussion sections in reports of controlled trials published in general medical journals. *JAMA* **287**, 2799–801.

Constantini, N.W., Dubnov, G. and Lebrun, C.M. (2005) The menstrual cycle and sport performance. *Clin Sports Med* **24**(2), e51–82, xiii–xiv.

Corbett, J., Barwood, M.J. and Parkhouse, K. (2009) Effect of task familiarisation on distribution of energy during a 2000 m cycling time trial. *Br J Sports Med* **43**, 770–4.

Coughlan, M., Cronin, P. and Ryan, F. (2007) Step-by-step guide to critiquing research. Part 1: quantitative research. *Br J Nurs* **16**(11), 658–63.

Creme, P. and Lea, M.R. (2006) *Writing at University: A Guide for Students*, 2nd edn. Maidenhead: Open University Press.

Crowe, M. and Sheppard, L. (2011) A review of critical appraisal tools show they lack rigor: alternative tool structure is proposed. *J Clin Epidemiol* **64**(1), 79–89.

Crowe, M., Sheppard, L. and Campbell, A. (2011a) Comparison of the effects of using the Crowe Critical Appraisal Tool versus informal appraisal in assessing health research: a randomised trial. *Int J Evid Based Healthc* **9**(4), 444–9. doi: 10.1111/j.1744-1609.2011.00237.x.

Crowe, M., Sheppard, L. and Campbell, A. (2011b) Reliability analysis for a proposed critical appraisal tool demonstrated value for diverse research designs. *J Clin Epidemiol* [epub ahead of print].

Damavandi, M., Dixon, P.C. and Pearsall, D.J. (2011) Ground reaction force adaptations during cross-slope walking and running. *Hum Mov Sci* [epub ahead of print].

Day, R.A. (1998) *How to Write and Publish a Scientific Paper*. Cambridge: Cambridge University Press; Phoenix, AZ: Oryx Press.

Deane, M. (2010) *Academic Research, Writing and Referencing: Inside track*. Harlow: Pearson Education.

Domholdt, E. Flaherty. J.L. and Phiilips, J.M. (1994) Critical appraisal of research literature by expert and inexperienced physical therapy researchers. *Phys Therapy* **74**(9), 853–60.

Drust, B., Reilly, T. and Cable, N.T. (2000) Physiological responses to laboratory-based soccer-specific intermittent and continuous exercise. *J Sports Sci* **18**(11), 885–92.

Durnin, J.V. and Womersley, J. (1974) Body fat assessed from total body density and its estimation from skinfold thickness: measurements on 481 men and women aged from 16 to 72 years. *Br J Nutr* **32**(1), 77–97.

Eston, R.G. and Rowlands, A.V. (2000) Stages in the development of a research project: putting the idea together. *Br J Sports Med* **34**(1), 59–64. Review.

Fallowfield, J.L., Williams, C., Booth, J., Choo, B.H. and Growns, S. (1996) Effect of water ingestion on endurance capacity during prolonged running. *J Sports Sci* **14**(6), 497–502.

Foote, M. (2006a) How to make a good first impression: a proper introduction. *Chest* **130**(6), 1935–7.

Foote, M. (2006b) Some concrete ideas about manuscript abstracts. *Chest* **129**(5), 1375–7.

Foote, M. (2007) Why references: giving credit and growing the field. *Chest* **132**(1), 344–6.

Foote, M. (2008) Materials and methods: a recipe for success. *Chest* **133**(1), 291–3.

Foote, M. (2009a) Backing up your statements: how to perform literature searches to prove your points. *Chest* **136**(5), 1432–4.

Foote, M. (2009b) The proof of the pudding: how to report results and write a good discussion. *Chest* **135**(3), 866–8.

Gaafar, R. (2005) How to write an oncology manuscript. *J Egyptian Nat Cancer Inst* **17**(3), 132–8.

Gaitanos, G.C., Nevill, M.E., Brooks, S. and Williams, C. (1991) Repeated bouts of sprint running after induced alkalosis. *J Sports Sci* **9**(4), 355–70.

Green, B.N., Johnson, C.D. and Adams, A. (2001) Writing narrative literature reviews for peer-reviewed journals: secrets of the trade. *J Sports Chiropr Rehabil* **15**, 5–19.

Greenhalgh, T. (1997) How to read a paper: getting your bearings (deciding what the paper is about). *BMJ* **315**, 243–6.

Hall, S.J. (1999) *Basic Biomechanics*, 3rd edn. Boston, MA and London: McGrawHill, pp. 398–401.

Hall, P.A. (2011) Getting your paper published: an editor's perspective. *Ann Saudi Med* **31**(1), 72–6.

Hamilton, A.L., Nevill, M.E., Brooks, S. and Williams, C. (1991) Physiological responses to maximal intermittent exercise: differences between endurance-trained runners and games players. *J Sports Sci* **9**(4), 371–82.

Hardy, S. and Ramjeet, J. (2005) Reflections on how to write and organise a research thesis. *Nurse Res* **13**(2), 27–39.

Harriss, D.J. and Atkinson, G. (2009) International Journal of Sports Medicine – ethical standards in sport and exercise science research. *Int J Sports Med* **30**, 701–2.

Hart, C. (1998) *Doing a Literature Review: Releasing the Social Science Research Imagination*. London: Sage.

Hartley, J. (2000) Clarifying the abstracts of systematic literature reviews. *Bull Med Libr Assoc* **88**(4), 332–7.

Hartley, J. (2004) Current findings from research on structured abstracts. *J Med Libr Assoc* **92**(3), 268–371.

Helgerud, J., Høydal, K., Wang, E., Karlsen, T., Berg, P., Bjerkaas, M., Simonsen, T., Helgesen, C., Hjorth, N., Bach, R. and Hoff, J. (2007) Aerobic high-intensity intervals improve VO_{2max} more than moderate training. *Med Sci Sports Exerc* **39**, 665–71.

Heller, R.F., Verma, A., Gemmell, I., Harrison, R., Hart, J. and Edwards, R. (2008) Critical appraisal for public health: a new checklist. *Public Health* **122**(1), 92–8.

Hertel, J. (2010) Keep it simple: study design nomenclature in research article abstracts. *J Athl Train* **45**(3), 213–14.

Hopkins, W.G., Hawley, J.A. and Burke, L.M. (1999) Design and analysis of research on sport performance enhancement. *Med Sci Sports Exerc* **31**(3), 472–85.

Hopkins, W.G., Marshall, S.W., Batterham, A.M. and Hanin, J. (2009) Progressive statistics for studies in sports medicine and exercise science. *Med Sci Sports Exerc* **41**(1), 3–13. Review.

Huwiler-Müntener, K., Jüni, P., Junker, C. and Egger, M. (2002) Quality of reporting of randomized trials as a measure of methodologic quality. *JAMA* **287**(21), 2801–4.

Hyman, R. (1995) How to critique a published article. *Psychol Bull* **118**, 178–82.

International Committee of Medical Journal Editors (1997) Uniform requirements for manuscripts submitted to biomedical journals. *N Engl J Med* **336**(4), 309–15.

Janse de Jonge, X.A. (2003) Effects of the menstrual cycle on exercise performance. *Sports Med* **33**(11), 833–51.

Jones, A.M. and Doust, J.H. (1996) A 1% treadmill grade most accurately reflects the energetic cost of outdoor running. *J Sports Sci* **14**(4), 321–7.

Kallet, R.H. (2004) How to write the methods section of a research paper. *Respir Care* **49**(10), 1229–32.

Karaba-Jakovljević, D., Popadić-Gaćesa, J., Grujić, N., Barak, O. and Drapsin, M. (2007) Motivation and motoric tests in sports. *Med Pregl* **60**(5–6), 231–6.

Katch, V.L., Sady, S.S. and Freedson, P. (1982) Biological variability in maximum aerobic power. *Med Sci Sports Exerc* **14**(1), 21–5.

Knight, K.L. (2010) Study/experimental/research design: much more than statistics. *J Athletic Training* **45**(1), 98–100.

Kyrgidis, A. and Triaridis, S. (2010) Methods and biostatistics: a concise guide for peer reviewers. *Hippokratia* **14**(Suppl 1), 13–22.

Lebrun, C.M. (1994) The effect of the phase of the menstrual cycle and the birth control pill on athletic performance. *Clin Sports Med* **13**(2), 419–41.

Livingstone, S.D., Nolan, R.W. and Cattroll, S.W. (1989) Heat loss caused by immersing the hands in water. *Aviat Space Environ Med* **60**(12), 1166–71.

Lynch, C. (2010) *Doing Your Research Project in Sport*. London: Sage.

MacAuley, D. (1994) READER: an acronym to aid critical reading by general practitioners. *Br J Gen Pract* **44**(379), 83–5.

MacAuley, D. (1996) Critical reading using the READER acronym at an international workshop. *Fam Pract* **13**(1), 104–5.

MacAuley, D. and McCrum, E. (1999) Critical appraisal using the READER method: a workshop-based controlled trial. *Fam Pract* **16**(1), 90–3.

MacAuley, D., McCrum, E. and Brown, C. (1998) Randomised controlled trial of the READER method of critical appraisal in general practice. *BMJ* **316**(7138), 1134–7.

MacAuley, D. and Sweeney, K.G. (1997) Critical reading using the READER acronym by experienced general practitioners (GPs) and by GP registrars in southern and Northern Ireland. *Ir J Med Sci* **166**(3), 121–3.

Maher, C.G., Sherrington, C., Elkins, M., Herbert, R.D. and Mosele, A.M. (2004) Challenges for evidence-based physical therapy: accessing and interpreting high-quality evidence on therapy. *Physical Therapy* **84**(7).

Marino, F.E., Kay, D., Cannon, J., Serwach, N. and Hilder, M. (2002) A reproducible and variable intensity cycling performance protocol for warm conditions. *J Sci Med Sport* **5**(2), 95–107.

Marks, C. and Katch, V. (1986) Biological and technological variability of residual lung volume and the effect on body fat calculations. *Med Sci Sports Exerc* **18**(4), 485–8.

Maughan, R.J., Greenhaff, P.L., Leiper, J.B., Ball, D., Lambert, C.P. and Gleeson, M. (1997) Diet composition and the performance of high-intensity exercise. *J Sports Sci* **15**(3), 265–75.

Maughan, R., Nevill, A., Boreham, C., Davison, R., Linthorne, N., Stewart, A., Williams, M. and Winter, E. (2007) Ethical issues when submitting to the Journal of Sports Sciences. *J Sports Sci* **25**(6), 617–18.

McGawley, K. and Bishop, D. (2006) Reliability of a 5 × 6-s maximal cycling repeated-sprint test in trained female team-sport athletes. *Eur J Appl Physiol* **98**(4), 383–93.

McNair, P.J., Depledge, J., Brettkelly, M. and Stanley, S.N. (1996) Verbal encouragement: effects on maximum effort voluntary muscle action. *Br J Sports Med* **30**(3), 243–5.

McNamee, M., Olivier, S. and Wainwright, P. (2007) *Research Ethics in Exercise, Health and Sports Science*, 116–20. London: Routledge.

Moher, D., Liberati, A., Tetzlaff, J. and Altman, D.G. (2009) Preferred reporting items for systematic reviews and meta-analyses: the PRISMAstatement. *BMJ* **339**, 2535. doi: 10.1136/bmj.b2535.

Morris, J.G., Nevill, M.E. and Williams, C. (2000) Physiological and metabolic responses of female games and endurance athletes to prolonged, intermittent, high-intensity running at 30 degrees and 16 degrees C ambient temperatures. *Eur J Appl Physiol* **81**(1–2), 84–92.

Morris, J.G., Nevill, M.E., Boobis, L.H., Macdonald, I.A. and Williams, C. (2005) Muscle metabolism, temperature, and function during prolonged, intermittent, high-intensity running in air temperatures of 33 degrees and 17 degrees C. *Int J Sports Med* **26**(10), 805–14.

Nevill, A. (2000) Just how confident are you when publishing the results of your research? *J Sports Sci* **18**(8), 569–70.

Neville, C. (2007) *The Complete Guide to Referencing and Avoiding Plagiarism.* London: Open University Press, McGraw-Hill Education.

Ng, K.H. and Peh, W.C.G. (2010a) Writing a systematic review. *Singapore Med J* **51**(5), 362–5.

Ng, K.H. and Peh, W.C.G. (2010b) Writing the materials and methods. *Singapore Med J* **49**(11), 856–8.

Nicholas, C.W., Nuttall, F.E. and Williams, C. (2000) The Loughborough Intermittent Shuttle Test: a field test that simulates the activity pattern of soccer. *J Sports Sci* **18**(2), 97–104.

Noble, B.J. and Robertson, R.J. (1996) *Perceived Exertion.* Champaign, IL: Human Kinetics.

Ntoumadis, N. (2001) *A Step-By-Step Guide to SPSS for Sport and Exercise Studies.* London: Routledge.

Nurmekivi, A., Karu, T., Pihl, E., Jürimäe, T. and Lemberg, H. (2001) Blood lactate recovery and perceived readiness to start a new run in middle-distance runners during interval training. *Percept Mot Skills* **93**(2), 397–404.

O'Toole, M.L., Hiller, D.B., Crosby, L.O. and Douglas, P.S. (1987) The ultraendurance triathlete: a physiological profile. *Med Sci Sports Exerc* **19**(1), 45–50.

Pamir, M.N. (2002) How to write an experimental research paper. *Acta Neurochir Suppl* **83**, 109–13.

Peh, W.C.G. and Ng, K.H. (2008) Abstract and keywords. *Singapore Med J* **49**(9), 664–5.

Peh, W.C.G. and Ng, K.H. (2010) Writing an invited review. *Singapore Med J* **51**(4), 271–3.

Pitsiladis, Y.P. and Maughan, R.J. (1999) The effects of exercise and diet manipulation on the capacity to perform prolonged exercise in the heat and in the cold in trained humans. *J Physiol* **517**(3), 919–30.

Price, M.J. and Campbell, I.G. (1997) Thermoregulatory responses of able-bodied and paraplegic athletes to prolonged upper body exercise. *Euro J Appl Phys,* **76**: 552–60.

Price, M.J. and Campbell, I.G. (1999) Thermoregulatory responses of spinal cord injured and able-bodied athletes to prolonged upper body exercise and recovery. *Spinal Cord* **37**(11), 772–9.

Price, M. and Halabi, K. (2005) The effects of work-rest duration on intermittent exercise and subsequent performance. *J Sports Sci* **23**(8), 835–42.

Ramanathan, N.L. (1964) A new weighting system for mean surface temperature of the human body. *J Appl Phys* **19**, 531–3.

Reilly, T. (2007) Circadian Rhythms. In E.M. Winter, A.M. Jones, R.C.R. Davidson, P.D. Bromley and T.H. Mercer (eds.), *Sport and Exercise Physiology Testing Guidelines,* 54–60. Abingdon: Routledge.

Ridley, D. (2008) *The Literature Review. A Step by Step Guide for Students.* London: Sage.

Rozenek, R., Funato, K., Kubo, J., Hoshikawa, M. and Matsuo, A. (2007) Physiological responses to interval training sessions at velocities associated with VO_{2max}. *J Strength Cond Res* **21**, 188–92.

Ryall, E. (2010) *Critical Thinking for Sports Students.* Exeter: Learning Matters.

Ryan, F., Coughlan, M. and Cronin, P. (2007) Step-by-step guide to critiquing research. Part 2: qualitative research. *Br J Nurs* **16**(12), 738–44. Review.

Sandelowski, M. (2008) Reading, writing and systematic review. *J Adv Nurs* **64**(1), 104–10.

Sanderson, F.H. and Reilly, T. (1983) Trait and state anxiety in male and female cross-country runners. *Br J Sports Med* **17**(1), 24–6.

Sealey, R.M., Spinks, W.L., Leicht, A.S. and Sinclair, W.H. (2010) Identification and reliability of pacing strategies in outrigger canoeing ergometry. *J Sci Med Sport* **13**, 241–6.

Seals, D.R. and Tanaka, H. (2000) Manuscript peer review: a helpful checklist for students and novice referees. *Adv Physiol Educ* **23**(1), 52–8.

Seiler, S. and Hetlelid, K.J. (2005) The impact of rest duration on work intensity and RPE during interval training. *Med Sci Sports Exerc* **37**, 1601–7.

Sewell, D.A. and McGregor, R.A. (2008) Evaluation of a cycling pre-load time trial protocol in recreationally active humans. *Eur J Appl Physiol* **102**(5), 615–21.

Siri, W.E. (1961) Body composition from fluid space and density. In J. Brozek and A. Hanschel (eds.), *Techniques for Measuring Body Composition*, 223–44. Washington, DC: National Academy of Science.

Skelton, J. (1994) Analysis of the structure of original research papers: an aid to writing original papers for Publication. *Br J Gen Pract* **44**, 455–9.

Skelton, J.R. and Edwards, S.J. (2000) The function of the discussion section in academic medical writing. *BMJ* **320**, 1269–70.

Smith, P.M., Doherty, M., Drake, D., Price, M.J. (2004) The influence of step and ramp type protocols on the attainment of peak physiological responses during arm crank ergometry. *Int J Sports Med* **25**(8), 616–21.

Smith, P.M. and Price, M.J. (2007) Upper-body exercise. In E.M. Winter, A.M. Jones, R.C.R. Davidson, P.D. Bromley and T.H. Mercer (eds.), *Sport and Exercise Physiology Testing Guidelines*, 138–44. Abingdon: Routledge.

Speed, H.D. and Andersen, M.B. (2000) What exercise and sport scientists don't understand. *J Sci Med Sport* **3**(1), 84–92.

Spencer, M., Fitzsimons, M., Dawson, B., Bishop, D. and Goodman, C. (2006) Reliability of a repeated-sprint test for field-hockey. *J Sci Med Sport* **9**, 181–4.

Squires, B.P. (1990) Structured abstracts of original research and review articles. *Can Med Assoc J* **143**(7), 619–22.

Sunderland, C. and Nevill, M. (2003) Effect of the menstrual cycle on performance of intermittent, high-intensity shuttle running in a hot environment. *Eur J Appl Physiol* **88**(4–5), 345–52.

Sunderland, C. and Nevill, M.E. (2005) High-intensity intermittent running and field hockey skill performance in the heat. *J Sports Sci* **23**(5), 531–40.

Suriano, R., Edge, J. and Bishop, D. (2010) Effects of cycle strategy and fibre composition on muscle glycogen depletion pattern and subsequent running economy. *Br J Sports Med* **44**(6), 443–8.

Svedenhag, J. and Sjödin, B. (1985) Maximal and submaximal oxygen uptakes and blood lactate levels in elite male middle- and long-distance runners. *Int J Sports Med* **5**(5), 255–61.

Thomas, J.R. and Nelson, J.K. (2001) *Research Methods in Physical Activity*, 4th edn. Champaign, IL: Human Kinetics.

Thompson, A. and Taylor, B.N. (2008) *The International System of Units*. NIST Special Publication 330. Gaithersburg, MD: National Institute of Science and Technology.

Turk, C. and Kirkman, J. (1989) *Effective Writing: Improving Scientific Technical and Business Communication*. London: Spon.

Tyler, C. and Sunderland, C. (2009) The effect of ambient temperature on the reliability of a preloaded treadmill time-trial. *Int J Sports Med* **29**, 812–16.

Vincent, W.J. (1999) *Statistics in Kinesiology*, 2nd edn. Champaign, IL: Human Kinetics.

Wells, W.A. (2006) Unpleasant surprises: how the Introduction has wandered into the Discussion. *J Cell Biol*, **174**(6), 741.

Wieseler, B. and McGauran, N. (2010) Reporting a systematic review. *Chest* **137**(5), 1240–6.

Winter, E. (2005) Writing: Bartlett revisited. *J Sports Sci* **23**(8), 773.

Winter, E.M. and Maughan, R.J. (2009) Requirements for ethics approvals. *J Sports Sci* **27**(10), 985.

Young, A.J., Sawka, M.N., Epstein, Y, Decristofano, B. and Pandolf, K.B. (1987) Cooling different body surfaces during upper and lower body exercise. *J Appl Phys* **63**, 1218–23.

Young, J.M. and Solomon, M.J. (2009) How to critically appraise an article. *Nat Clin Pract Gastroenterol Hepatol* **6**, 82–91. doi: 10.1038/ncpgasthep1331.

Index